The Journey
of
My Life

BRANKO FRANOVICK

Copyright © 2024 Branko Franovick
All rights reserved
First Edition

Fulton Books
Meadville, PA

Published by Fulton Books 2024

ISBN 979-8-89221-949-5 (paperback)
ISBN 979-8-89221-950-1 (digital)

Printed in the United States of America

I dedicate this book to my wife, Vera, son Michael, and daughter-in-law Rani. You mean the world to me.

I was born on March 1, 1940, in the village named Katun, near Petrovac, in the then-state of Montenegro, country Yugoslavia. These were turbulent times when the occupying forces of Germany and Italy were stumping the grounds of Balkan nations. In those villages along the coast of the Adriatic Sea were mostly peasants with very little farming land and had to struggle for survival.

Mostly, from every family, one person would go to work in foreign countries, such as the United States and Canada, to work in mines and steel mills or any other unskilled work to earn some money to send back home and to help their families survive hard times.

One of those people was my uncle Spiro, who sailed on a ship back in the 1920s to work as a merchant marine, not knowing where he was going or what his future would be. After a number of years of sailing to different countries and continents, he found himself in Panama City, Panama. He worked there for a while, mostly in the restaurants, until authorities discovered that he was an illegal immigrant and wanted to deport him back to his homeland. He knew that deportation would mean never coming back to that part of the world, so to avoid that situation, he told the authorities that he missed his family and that he wanted to purchase a ticket to go back home. That he did: purchased a ticket for the ship that was sailing to Europe via New York City. His goal was that the first opportunity he got would leave the ship and continue to stay in the Western world. When he reached New York City, somehow, he got on shore and did not return to the ship, as they were saying those days, "Jumped the ship." Being an illegal resident, he had a very hard time finding a job and had to be on the lookout all the time not to be discovered or reported to the authorities to face another deportation. Most of his work was in the restaurants and hospital laundry rooms.

In 1937, working in the Mount Sinai Hospital, he met a young woman named Maria, from Czechoslovakia, with the status of a legal resident of the United States. They got to know each other very well, as they had many things in common. Being from Europe and having the similarity of a Slavish language, they could easily communicate with each other.

Maria had a large family: three sisters and a brother, Sidi, Elsa, Hilda, and Gustav. Spiro, they called him Steve, got quickly liked by all of them and made him feel as if it was his own family. Shortly after that, they got married. Whether that was instant love or convenience, it worked for them for fifty-five years to the rest of their lives.

They were working hard to save some money with the hope of buying a home. Steve was still facing difficulties of being illegal and not able to get a better-paying job to get quicker ahead with his dreams. At about this time in Europe, World War II was looming on the horizon, and the United States was near entering the war. The massive

THE JOURNEY OF MY LIFE

buildup of arms and troops was underway, so young Steve saw the opportunity to join the army, get legal status, and solve his immigration problem once and for all. The recruiting officer did not ask many questions as they were glad to sign up anyone who wished to volunteer for the duty in the arm forces and possibilities to be sent to the war front.

Steve joined the Army and immediately was sent to basic training at Fort Drum, New York, located near the Canadian border. During the training there, the drill sergeant discovered that Steve was not a citizen and that he also did not have proof of legal entry to the United States. No person could be sent to the war zone without being a citizen of the United States, so Steve once again found himself facing an immigration problem.

The commanding officer was very sympathetic to his problem and gave him an overnight pass to cross into Canada and, on return, to have his papers stamped and dated at the border crossing so they could legally establish his entry to the United States. Upon his return, Steve was sworn in and became a citizen of the United States, served in the Army, and got an honorable discharge. Upon return to civilian life, Steve sought a job with the United States post office in New York City and remained there until retirement.

During all this time of war years, Steve had no communication with the family in the old country, where destruction and the loss of life were to unimaginable proportions. Steve's family was not spared, learning that his younger brother Milos was killed in the war, leaving behind a newborn and never-seen son, Branko, and young wife, Stana,

Mother Kata, and unmarried sister, Milica, all living in the village Katun, near Petrovac, Montenegro. Milos also left behind brother Simo in Petrovac, brother Andrija in Herceg-Novi, and sister Andja in Belgrade.

At the very beginning of World War II, my father, Milos, joined partisans in the fight against German and Italian occupying forces that were terrorizing our people and destroying everything in their sight. It was just after he got married and before my birth that my father, Milos, left behind his family and proudly joined many other countrymen to take the fight to the occupiers, wherever it may be, knowing that he may never come back home alive. The war was raging all over Yugoslavia, and the partisans without adequate arms and supplies had to face a well-equipped enemy.

It was recorded in the history books, from the memoirs of a local war hero, Marko Statistic, about my father's heroism against the enemy invaders as well as home traitors. Early in the war, in the high mountains of Montenegro, he was wounded but did not want to return home. Instead, he chose to continue fighting until the end of his life. On June 10, 1943, in Balinovac, mountain Zelengora, my father was killed in the attack against the German machine gun position. He was a great patriot, and I am very proud of him. I was three and a half years old when we got the news that my father was killed in the war, and I remember well my mother and the rest of the family were screaming and crying. I was too young to understand what was happening, but one thing was for sure, my life from that moment on would change forever.

THE JOURNEY OF MY LIFE

The war was still raging on, and I remember seeing four-engine warplanes dropping bombs in the Adriatic Sea. I was scared, and in my young mind, I did not know why they were doing that. In later years, adults were describing how the allied warplanes were bombing enemy positions inland, and unused bombs had to be dropped somewhere for safe landing, and to save the civilian population, the leftover bombs were dropped in the Adriatic Sea. Later, the adults told these and many other war stories and their horror experiences that they had to go through the war years.

Right after the war, our people in the village, in Montenegro, and the country of Yugoslavia as a whole had to go through a very difficult time of healing the wounds despite the heavy loss of life and destruction. For any child, growing up under these conditions would be hard to imagine what the future will hold.

In my home, I was the only child living with my mother, aunt, and grandmother. At a very young age, the feeling of not having a father started setting in, and it was only the beginning of what was coming down the road for me and my future. It was almost time for me to go to school. During the war, our local school was burned down to the ground by Italian soldiers, so the school was temporarily set up in a private home so the children could get some education. I was six years old, and I remember very well my first day of school, sharing a very small bench with my cousin Slavomir. For the following three years, we continued going to this temporary school in a private home. During the fourth and final elementary school year, I finished in a newly rebuilt school.

Looking back at those years and considering all surrounding conditions, such as not having even the most necessities of food and clothing, the children were very bright and eager to learn. The next step was the beginning of middle school in Petrovac, which was three kilometers away from home in the village. This meant walking every day to and from school, rain or shine. Despite all the harsh weather and long distances to school, we were striving to achieve good results. Also, the credit had to be given to excellent teachers, who had special gifts and understanding of how to elevate the minds of young students and how to prepare them for the next face of studies and guidance to a better life in the future. I liked my teachers, and I think they made a lifelong impression on me, and the knowledge I acquired in those days helped me to better propel through the good and bad times of my life.

My uncle Steve from America was helping us by sending money and packages of clothes so we could survive the hard times. In the household, no one worked, so there was no income other than help from my uncle Steve.

Growing up without a father was very difficult for me, but now I was facing another misfortune in my life. My mother was romantically involved with a man from the village nearby and wanted to remarry and take me with her.

In those days, her behavior was considered shameful and not acceptable. At the time, I was only twelve years old when I made my firm decision that I wanted to remain in my father's house with my aunt Milica and grandmother Kate.

My mother's actions hurt me deeply, and God only knows how I felt and how many tears I shed, but life went on as I continued going to school and facing more responsibilities each day.

Living in the village had many challenges. The houses did not have electricity or running water. For the light, we were using kerosene burning lamps, and for the water, we had to go outside to a centrally located place for the use of the entire village. In 1931, our fathers built a water reservoir and a special place where the animals could drink water and our mothers could wash clothes. The electricity did not come to our village until 1955, and I remember that my house was the first one to receive the installation. The electricity brought us joy, happiness, and many other things to improve our lives. Shortly after that, I had the first radio in the village, and from there on, we were so-called connected to the world.

It was sometime in my middle school days when my uncle Steve sent us a letter telling us that he would like to bring me to the United States. I was very happy to hear that, thinking that I would be going very soon, not knowing what was needed for this kind of process and how long it would take. This was a communist country, and the quota system for exiting the country was very tight; in fact, it took a lot of patience, money, and connections over the next five years to get a Yugoslav passport and entry visa to the United States. My aunt Milica obtained on my behalf all the necessary documents and applied for the issuance of a passport, which was needed first to apply for a US entry visa. We were told that it would take some time but not to worry, everything will be fine. In the meantime, I continued to go to school and tried to cope with the situation as best I could. On the surface, it seemed very simple, but my life from that time on changed dramatically, affecting my studies, relationships with friends, and, in general, whatever I was doing, the thought of going to America followed me day and night. The people were very sympathetic to me. Knowing my situation of growing up without a mother and father helped me in many ways.

I was spending lots of time with my cousins and other children in the village, but among all of them, Vladimir was my best friend. Vladimir had two older sisters, and Vera was the youngest one, four years younger than me. Whenever possible, I tried to be with them, in their house or whatever chores they had to do. There was something special about Vera. Even at that age, I was looking forward to being around her wherever she was. As a child, she was a very closed person and never revealed her feelings about me, but that did not stop me from pursuing our friendship. These were much more different times; the relationships were more secretive, but the feelings were nurtured and treasured forever. These early feelings about Vera had a special place in my heart, and there is a lot more to come.

My life was getting more complicated by the day. Growing up without parents, schoolwork, thoughts about going to America, and now developing feelings about girls was a lot more on my plate than I could digest.

Time went by, and there was no word on my passport application, which made me feel that something was not going well. Post-wartime, Yugoslavia was a communist country and did not like to see young men immigrating to the Western world, so my passport application got caught up in bureaucratic procedures not allowing me to immigrate. Realizing that my dream of going to America may be in jeopardy, I turned back my focus on studying and finishing middle school. After completing middle school, I had a choice of going to high school or trade school. My desire was to work with wood, and I selected to go to the trade school for fine carpentry and cabinetmaking. The nearest school of this kind was in Kotor, some fifty kilometers away from home. On September 1, 1957, I went to Kotor, registered in the trade school, rented the room that I coshared with a friend to make it more affordable, and signed up for the meals at a student cafeteria. The school program was structured in such a way as to work five hours daily in the furniture factory with the assigned instructor and, after lunch, attend a classroom for three hours. This was an excellent three-year program, with learning combination of theoretical in the classroom and hands-on practical shop experience.

For me, living in Kotor was very much different from living in the village. It did not take me long to adjust because the people in Kotor were very nice, and I had many friends. Very often, my thoughts were wandering back home and thinking about everything there. Vera was still going to Petrovac in middle school, so I did not get to see her much. In my school, I was doing very well, which eased my thinking about getting a passport to America.

I made another attempt to find out what was going on with my passport application, and the answer was the same as before: it is in the process. Now for the first time, I understood that getting the passport was not going to happen. Shortly before this time, my older cousin, Savo Franovic, was appointed director of a newly built, very luxurious Hotel Metropol in Belgrade, the capital of Yugoslavia. With a prestigious job like that, I thought he may have important friends in high government positions and may be able to help me in getting the passport. Sure enough, he had a friend, Mr. Aleksandar Rankovic, who was the number three most important person in the government of Yugoslavia, and Savo told me to come to Belgrade so he could personally take me to Mr. Rankovic. I was very happy to hear that, and my hopes were raised again that, finally, someone would help me with obtaining the passport.

    Those days, it was not simple to travel to Belgrade. I had to take a bus to Zelenika, a town near Herceg-Novi, and take a small narrow track (Ciro) train to Sarajevo, where I changed to an express train for Belgrade. It took two days of travel, and I felt very courageous to pull this off, as I have never been this far away from home. My aunt Andjelika was living in Belgrade, so I stayed with her while I was there. I contacted my cousin Savo to let him know that I arrived in Belgrade and to see when we could meet. Savo made an appointment, and we were all set to see his friend.

    Mr. Aleksandar Rankovic was a very important man in charge of all the intelligence for the country, so one can imagine how hard it was for me to appear before this very powerful man and practically beg him to allow me to leave the country. Finally, Savo and I went to Mr. Rankovic's office, and I found him everything else but what I expected.

He was very kind and acted very friendly, which put me at ease. After a small chat with Savo, he asked me why I wanted to leave Yugoslavia. I was a little shaky at first, but I pulled myself together and explained how I lost my father in the war, that my mother remarried, and that my uncle Steve did not have children of his own, so he and his wife wanted to help me by bringing me to America.

Mr. Rankovic did not say much after that but thanked me for coming and said that everything would be fine. I returned to Kotor to continue my school. Shortly after that, I was notified by the local authority that my passport was issued, and it was valid until December 15, 1959. Now the pressure was on me again, as I knew very well that if I did not receive an entry visa for the United States before my passport expired, I would be drafted into the Yugoslav army, and that would be the end of my dreams of leaving the country. To make a better case in applying for a permanent entry visa to the US, my Uncle Steve suggested that he and his wife adopt me.

As I was still under the age, my mother agreed to that, and we went back to my cousin Savo to help us expedite adoption papers. Now that I had my passport, adoption papers, and all other necessary documents, I went to the American embassy in Belgrade to apply for my entry visa to the United States. The embassy had heavy quota procedures, and there was no assurance that a visa would be granted anytime soon.

Once again, I returned to Kotor and continued the school that I loved very much. Whenever possible, on the weekend, I would go home in the village to my aunt Milica.

She loved me as if I were her own son; she cared for me, and her whole life was wrapped up all around me. Coming home also meant seeing Vera. She was near finishing middle school in Petrovac and very soon had to make the decision of where to enroll in high school. We did not have much communication those days, but I never stopped thinking about her, even though I had many other friends and girls too. For some reason, in my thoughts, I was always comparing other girls with Vera, not even knowing where that was leading me in future relations.

Back in the States, my uncle Steve wrote a letter to a new, very influential Republican, United States senator Jacob Javits from New York, to ask him for help in obtaining my entry visa. So far, everything possible was done, and the only thing left was to be patient and wait for the results. During that time, in the United States, there were more cases of adopted children like me wanting to come to their relatives in America, and senators from other states were working on their behalf.

On September 9, 1959, the US senators put together a joint resolution to facilitate the admission into the United States of certain aliens, of which I was one. This was Private Law 86-152 of Eighty-Sixth Congress, H. J. Res. 406. When this bill passed through the House and Senate, it was signed into law by President Dwight D. Eisenhower. Shortly after that, Senator Jacob Javits sent a telegram to my uncle Steve in New York, informing him that the embassy in Belgrade would be notified of this new law and that I would be granted an entry visa to the United States.

That same year, Vera came to Kotor, enrolled in the high school, and coshared a room with another girl from Petrovac. Unfortunately, I was strung between many different priorities facing me at that time, so I did not make more effort to see Vera and spend some time with her. I regret that to this very day.

That year, our trade school from Kotor was taking students on an excursion trip to Belgrade and Zagreb. I signed up for the trip together with my roommate and best friend, Mirko. I used this trip to go to Belgrade once again to stop at the US embassy and check on the progress of my visa. When I got to Belgrade, I went to the embassy, and to my surprise, I was told that they were about to contact me. I was requested to go to the designated physician for examination and blood screening. Every applicant in those days had to pass a clean bill of health to receive an entry visa. Now I knew that this process was nearing the end, and I returned to Kotor to notify my school and friends that I was finally leaving them for good. It was a very emotional goodbye that was a long time in the making, almost five years.

Back home in the village, my aunt Milica was bitter with the authorities for making it very difficult for me to emigrate sooner. It was hard for her to see me go, but she knew that it was good for me and my future, that I would not have it there.

Leaving behind home, relatives, friends, and everything I had to this point in my life did not come easy for me. Worst of all, I did not know how it would be where I was going and what was waiting for me in the new world where I would have to build my new future. Now I was nineteen years old, and by now, I have gone through so many experiences growing up that helped me better reason out where I come from and where I am going from here on.

Finally, I made my last trip to Belgrade before leaving Yugoslavia. This year, Vera's brother Vladimir, my best friend from childhood, enrolled in school at Belgrade, studying to be a teacher. I was happy to see him there, and we spent some time together. At the beginning of November 1959, the embassy issued my US entry visa, and now I was free to leave Yugoslavia anytime I wanted. Knowing that my passport was valid only until December 15, 1959, I decided to leave immediately that same day to take the train from Belgrade to Trieste, Italy. That evening, at the railroad station in Belgrade, I came to say goodbye to my best friend, Vladimir, and my aunt, Andjelika, who was living in Belgrade. I was so afraid that something may go wrong, so I did not want anyone else to know of my leaving. Once again, another emotional goodbye. I was on the way to Trieste, where I had to wait for the ship going to New York. The passengers on the train going to Trieste were put in the designated cars for Trieste, while other cars were to be disconnected at Zagreb. Those days in Yugoslavia had a shortage of just about everything, mostly clothing, so most of those people traveling with me were carrying with them bags full of meat products and cigarettes to sell in Italy to make some money for buying the clothing. The train was going fast, but the night seemed to be very long, and it took most of the next day to arrive at Trieste station. Now I realized that I was finally free from all my worries and difficulties that I had to go through for the last five years of my life.

As the train came to a halt, you could hear voices calling, "Sobe, sobe (rooms)," and as I was coming out of the train, one older gentleman approached me, in my language, and asked me if I needed a room to stay. I was very happy to hear that, and I told him that I needed a room for fifteen days. He took me and some other people from the train to his house, multirooms for rent. I had my own room, but some other people shared the rooms to save money. The people who came with me from the train were carrying bags full of smoked meat and cartons of cigarettes. What I observed was that the owner of the house was buying this stuff from them. I did not mix very much with those people, even though they spoke my language, because they were there only to shop and go back home. The owner's name was Ivan. He spoke my language and told me that he was from Croatia, and then I told him my situation, that I was waiting for the ship going to New York. Ivan and his wife were very nice to me, and they asked me to have breakfast with them every morning. After a few days, Ivan asked me if I could help him take some stuff to a restaurant across the town. I was very happy to go with him, as I had nothing else to do. Now I found out that the stuff we were carrying was meats and cartons of cigarettes that he purchased from the people who came with me on the train from Yugoslavia. I found out that in Italy, it was illegal to carry on the streets more than two cartons of cigarettes, and that was why Ivan asked me to go with him so we could double up on cigarettes. Apparently, Ivan had a deal with the restaurant to sell his goods. I offered myself to do this more often, and I ended up going alone to the restaurant two or three times a day for the rest of my stay in Trieste. Ivan and his wife trusted me with their dealings, and they were very appreciative of my help. Every day at the restaurant, I would get a free lunch or dinner with a glass of red wine. In the meantime, through the shipping agency, I had contact with my uncle Steve in New York, and he paid the agency $190 for my ticket from Trieste to New York City, leaving on December 5, 1959, on the ship *Vulcania*.

The trip was to take fifteen days, stopping in many countries on the way. On my final day of stay in Trieste, Ivan came with me to the pier to help me with boarding the ship and to make sure that I had no problem with the language. He was that kind of a caring person. I paid him for fifteen days' room charge. I had some extra lire left over, and I gave it all to him. He did not want to take it, but I forced him with an explanation that I would not need lire in America. He kissed me and wished me a good trip, and I boarded the ship.

On board the ship, I was guided to my cabin, which had four bunk beds. So far, I was the only one to occupy the cabin.

That afternoon of December 5, 1959, the ship *Vulcania* left the port of Trieste and sailed into the Adriatic Sea, heading toward the next port of Patras, Greece. Shortly after our departure, we had to go through a standard procedure of emergency drill, and immediately after, I started venturing around the ship to get familiar with where everything was. Sailing down the Adriatic, I knew that my Montenegro would be on the left side of the ship, so deep into the night, I got up and went on the outside deck to look toward the shores of my homeland. It was a very chilly and windy night, with a clear sky full of stars. The ship was too far from the shore for me to see anything, but I was leaning over as if I would be able to touch the shore. At that moment, I felt very lonely, and tears came down my face. I quickly realized that there was so much more for me to look forward to in the brighter days ahead. I had to overcome my feelings. I collected myself and returned to my cabin.

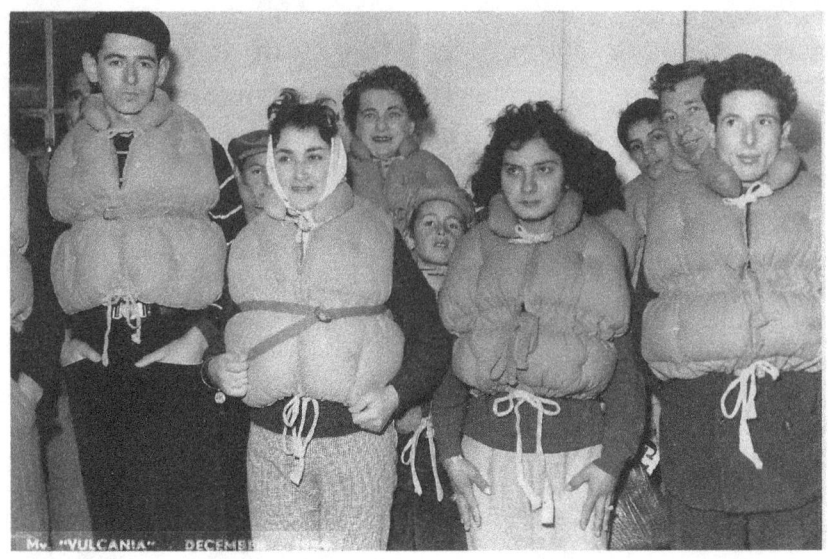

When we arrived in Patras, Greece, there were many passengers waiting to board the ship. I found out that some of those passengers were from neighboring countries, from Macedonia to Israel. One man with two boys from Israel was assigned to my cabin. The ship was not collecting only passengers but also mailing other goods along the way. The next port of call was Messina, Sicily. In each port, the ship was docked for several hours, so I was able to get on shore for sightseeing.

Now in the cabin, I had companions who spoke different languages, and we could not communicate very well. During the night, they would gather for a prayer session, and I did not know what was going on. One ship steward spoke my language, and I asked him if I could be transferred to another cabin. And with his help, I got moved to a cabin with two other people. After we left Patras, at the dinner table where I was assigned, came one family from

Macedonia and then Yugoslavia to share our table, which made me feel good to be with my countrymen. Every night at the dinner table, they would bring a jar of pickled hot peppers. The people from Balkan countries love hot peppers, so our new friends from Macedonia did not want to be without, even on a long journey like this one.

On the menu were mostly Italian dishes, served the family style, with a pitcher of red wine at every table. Next, we were coming up to the port of Messina, located in the Northern part of Sicily, near the boot of Italy. At each new port, there was something new to see, but mostly a lot of souvenir shops. The next port of call was Naples, located on the mainland of Italy. By now, we were five days into the trip, and I already had some friends, which made my trip more enjoyable.

In Naples, I spent the entire day with my friend from Macedonia, walking through the streets and comparing everything with back home in Yugoslavia. From Naples, we were sailing for Barcelona, Spain. This was the only port where I could not leave the ship with my passport because Yugoslavia, at that time, did not have diplomatic relations with Spain.

From Barcelona, we continued to our next destination of Gibraltar, where there was no pier to dock to, so the ship dropped anchor near the shore, where the new passengers and supplies arrived by tender. As I recall, there were so many small boats coming around the ship to sell souvenirs. If you were to buy something from those people, they would place it in the basket, lift it over to you on a long stick, and you return the money to them the same way. We did not spend much time there. We continued overnight sailing by the Rock of Gibraltar on the way to Lisbon, Portugal, where we spent an entire day. I went on shore with my Macedonian friend for sightseeing. We went on a hill overlooking the city. To this day, I treasure those beautiful memories from this gorgeous city, even though that was nearly sixty-four years ago. We left Lisbon in the evening hours on the way to Halifax, Canada, several days away.

Crossing the Atlantic Ocean this time of the year is a challenge for even larger ships. The *Vulcania* was an older ship, with a size of twenty-five thousand tons, and close to being put out of service. Nevertheless, we were sailing full steam ahead and challenging those steadily increasing waves. On the second day of our voyage from Lisbon, the weather was worsening, and we were getting information that ahead of us was a very dangerous storm. The ship captain announced that he was changing the course for some two hundred miles north to avoid the storm. During the night, the storm also changed the direction, unfortunately, our way, so sometime in the night, we were in the middle of a quite large and dangerous storm. The ship was going up and down, side by side, and everyone was fearful of what might happen. No one slept that night, and by morning, the waves were reduced somewhat, but it was still hard to move around the ship. I was seasick that night and did not show up for the meals the next day, but my friends brought me food in the cabin, hard-boiled eggs and bread to settle my stomach.

As the weather improved, so did my stomach too, and I was back in the dining room catching up on my lost calories. The travel was rather boring. On the outside deck, it was impossible to spend any time due to cold, wind, and rainy weather, so we mostly sat around and talked. Since the passengers were from different countries, they were hanging around in a group of their own nationality so they could communicate with each other. It was a mix of people of all ages, men and women, with very few children. I was mostly in the company of a family from Macedonia and two ladies from Croatia.

We arrived in Halifax, Nova Scotia, at midday. The two ladies from Croatia asked me to accompany them on shore as they wanted to visit the local church. I was very happy about the invitation; we disembarked the ship and went to look for the church. This was my first time to set foot on the soil of North America. We did not have to go very far, and as we were approaching the entrance to the church, one lady gave me ten cents to place on the icon in the church and to say the prayer with a wish of my importance. I grew up in a communist country, so I did not have much religious practice, but these ladies made me feel very comfortable to be with them. I walked up to a large icon on the side of the altar, placed my ten cents in the designated place for donations, and stared at the icon. My thoughts went immediately to my uncle and aunt in New York City, with a prayer to unite with them without any problems.

After the church, we walked through the streets before we returned to the ship. To my surprise, as I had never seen before, the Christmas decorations were all over the streets and homes. That made me feel wonderful. As the evening approached, the multicolor lights came on to make it even more spectacular. I guess this was the beginning of the many surprises to come in the new world. Back on the ship for overnight sailing to our next destination, New York City. The night seemed to be very long, as I felt a surge of anxiety, thinking all about tomorrow's meeting for the first time with my uncle Steve and aunt Maria. I got up in the dawn hours of the morning and went straight to the top deck of the ship. As we were approaching the New York Harbor, in the direction of the Hudson River, on the way to Manhattan's West Side docking piers, the heavy fag was lying low all over the entire area. Looking ahead in the distance, slightly to my left, I saw the top of a statue protruding through the fag, the best I could describe it, as a phenomenon, magical in every sense, and I could not get my eyes off it. Prior to coming there, I did not know anything about New York City. Later, I learned that it was the Statue of Liberty. Shortly ahead, we passed by Ellis Island, known for being the largest immigration processing center from 1892 to 1954. As the ship was docking, we were told to stay put until our name was called to disembark. For some reason, I was among the last passengers to be called. In the meantime, I was looking down at the pier to see if I could figure out which one of those people was my uncle Steve and aunt Maria. I had never seen their picture, so I did not know what they looked like. Fortunately, the pier was getting fewer people, so I spotted a man and woman pacing up and down the pier, which gave me an indication that it might be them. Finally, my name was called, and on the way out of the ship, those two people that I watched from the ship approached me, and now I knew for sure who they were. My uncle and aunt embraced me with happy tears, and finally, we got united. I envisioned my uncle to be a much older man, but he was only fifty-four years old and much younger looking than his age. From the pier, we took a taxi across Manhattan, then over the Queensboro Bridge to Jackson Heights, Queens. When we got to the house, I was surprised to see the house full of people. In fact, forty-two friends of my uncle and aunt were invited to welcome me and celebrate my arrival. They were my aunt's relatives, some neighbors, and my uncle's many friends from Yugoslavia. There were lots of glasses raised to welcome me, and we finished the evening with a dinner before everyone went to their homes. After this long and exhausting day, I was ready for some rest.

    The next day, the reality started setting in, so all the wishes and hopes to come to America were now behind me. From now on, it would be up to me to make something out of myself so my uncle and aunt would be proud of me. In the days ahead, my uncle did not stop asking questions about back home in the old country and telling me stories about his life. He was very happy, and I could tell that he loved me very much. Hilda, the youngest sister of my aunt Maria, lived only a few blocks away, and her daughter Ursula came to our house very often to help me learn English. One day, she told me that my name, Branko, was difficult to pronounce, and she gave me the nickname "Bill." So from that day on, everyone called me Bill, which suited me fine, as I did not have to spell it. One of my first priorities was to learn the English language, which would give me the opportunity to obtain a better job, and everything else would come easier. The high school in the neighborhood was offering at night specialized vocational courses, so I enrolled in the English language class. Also, with the help of television, movies, and newspapers, I was learning fast. Those days, the movie cost was twenty-five cents, and the most popular were the *Cowboy* movies.

My favorite place for the movies was in Manhattan, Times Square, at Forty-Second Street. My aunt Maria did not work, and most of the day, she was watching her television series, which looked to me alike. Slowly, I was getting impatient and wanted to start looking for a job. While in Yugoslavia, in the trade school, I acquired enough knowledge in carpentry, which made me confident that I could seek a job in that profession. In those days, the unions were very strong, and it was very difficult to get a job without the recommendation of a friend or family member of that trade union. Even so, my uncle was helping me to apply for a job in several places, but we did not have any success. My aunt Maria's nephew, who was working in a large metal stamping factory in Brooklyn, offered me if I would like to work there as an apprentice machinist. I was more than happy to get any job at any wage just to get out of the house, go to work, and learn English. This factory was Edwin B. Stimpson Company Inc., the largest eyelet and grommet manufacturer in the world.

On my first day, March 21, 1960, my uncle accompanied me to help me with English in filling out the work application. Everything worked out fine, and I started working immediately. The foreman took me around the department, introduced me to everyone, and then assigned me to a skilled worker to be his helper. In the department, many workers were immigrants from Europe, highly skilled, but some of them were not much better with English than I was. This was a metal stamping company producing eyelets, rivets, grommets, snap fasteners, and thousands of different metal parts for all kinds of industries. Also, the company was manufacturing attaching machines to set those products into various customer materials, such as fabric, leather, canvas, and so on. Each machine would be fitted with proper tooling for a particular item and size used. In our department, we were manufacturing the tooling for these machines for sale to a wide range of industries. At first, I was given orientation on working rules and regulations in the department, and then gradually, I was getting into the specifics of the work there. Perhaps the first several days were the most difficult, mostly because of the language barrier. The big help to all this was the friendliness of all, which gave me the feeling that this was one big family, even though there were over 350 employees in the company.

The office building was located on the corner of Franklin and Park Avenue, with the showroom on the first floor, exhibiting the samples of all the products, including attaching machines, and the floors above housing the sales office, accounting, payroll, executive offices, etc. There were other buildings behind the office building with different departments, such as the pressroom, tool and die, machine shop, finishing, heat treating, shipping, receiving, etc. Even across the street was a building for manufacturing rivets and hole plugs. Edwin B. Stimpson Company was established in 1852, privately owned and operated. From the very beginning, I got to like the company and the people working there. My starting wage was only one dollar per hour, with a twice-a-year automatic increase of five cents per hour. Even this low wage did not concern me because what I have seen so far gave me reason to believe that there would be plenty of opportunity for my advancement. On the home front, I did not have much social activity other than family gatherings for birthdays, holidays, etc. We are of the Eastern Orthodox Faith, and my uncle was a member of St. Sava, Serbian Orthodox Cathedral, located on Twenty-Fifth Street, downtown Manhattan. Next to the cathedral was a building used for social gatherings, where the Circle of Serbian Sisters would prepare delicious lunches to be served after church services. This was nice for parishioners to socialize, and it was especially good for me as a newcomer to meet more people. Through my uncle and his friends, in a very short time, I got to know everyone there. As time went by, my English was getting better, the work was progressing nicely, and it seemed that every new day was bringing something better than I expected. After several months of going to church, I met a girl named Olga from Yugoslavia. Olga was about my age, tall and very attractive, and also a newcomer to the United States. She lived outside the city and always came to the church with her mother. We became very good friends, and I got to know her very well. In the meantime, I was twenty years old, and my social life started picking up, so the next desire I had was to obtain a driver's license and eventually buy a car. I signed up for driver's lessons which enabled me to pass the test and obtain the license. With the help of my uncle, just six months after my arrival in the United States, I purchased my first used car, a 1956 Chevy, for the cost of $650.

That summer, my first trip outside the city was with my aunt and uncle to visit our friends from the old country, living in the Washington, DC area. Our friends took us on a tour of the city, where we saw the Congress and Senate and the National Mall, and we even went to Arlington, the National Cemetery. Many things I read about Washington, our nation's capital; fortunately, now I had the opportunity to witness all its greatness. This was one memorable weekend that will stay with me forever. My uncle's house was the type of townhouse on the Eighty-Eighth Street, off

Northern Boulevard, Jackson Heights. On the back of the houses was the service road, where each house had access to the garage that was detached from the house. Also, my uncle kept in the garage wine-making equipment, as he was making fifty to one hundred gallons of wine each year for home use and to give out to friends. Special grapes for winemaking were coming from California, packed in forty-two-pound woodboxes to a distributor in Corona, Flushing. In New York State, it was legal to make up to two hundred gallons of wine each year for home use only. I think we had one of the best homemade wines I ever tested. Coming from the shores of the Adriatic Sea, I was not accustomed to facing a lot of snow and harsh winters, so I had to get used to it in a hurry. On the way to work, I had to walk several city blocks to the subway in Jackson Heights and from the subway in Brooklyn about the same distance to the workplace. Despite the weather conditions, I made sure to be on time and never miss a day of work. This was 1960, the year of a presidential election, where a fierce campaign between Republican candidate Richard M. Nixon and Democratic candidate John F. Kennedy. Also, this was the year of a memorable United Nations meeting that Fidel Castro attended, and Nikita Khrushchev acted primitively by removing the shoe from his foot and started banging it on the table. Very much Cold War years, between East and West.

At that time, I did not have any preference as to what political party I would like to belong to. In any case, I was not a citizen yet, so I could not vote. Even so, I followed all the political speeches and debates. From the very beginning, I considered myself fortunate because I was able to sort out all that political rhetoric and form my own opinion in everything I read or heard. The election was so close that we did not know until the next day that John F. Kennedy became the thirty-fifth president of the United States.

At work, I learned so much in the process of making tooling, so the foreman liked my work and decided to let me have my own workstation, consisting of a "Hjorth Bench Lathe Machine." The sales office would prepare production orders and channel them down to the proper departments. The machine tool orders came to our department to be distributed by the foreman according to the size and complexity of the order. In the beginning, the foreman would give me smaller and easier orders to gradually build up my proficiency. It did not take me long before I was asking for bigger and more complex tool orders. At the completion of each order, the form had to be filed as to how much time was used to complete the order. There was a chart on the wall listing how much time could be charged for making different types of tools. I started studying the method of making those tools instead of just following the way I was taught. I came up with a certain procedure to make those tools much faster than anyone made it before. Now the foreman started giving me more complex tool orders that required the use of more sophisticated machines in the department. There was a lot to learn, not only how to make a certain tool but also what type of steel to use and what process of heat treating to put it through to produce the best quality tool for long-lasting wear and tear. As most workers were of European origin, everyone loved to watch and play soccer.

Sometimes, on the weekend, we would meet to play soccer on the old soccer field nearby. Also, the company had a bowling team that played once a week, so many of us would go to watch them play.

The social life was picking up in all directions. I even got friendly with the girl who was working in the sales department and who recently arrived from Austria. It was a coincidence that her brother-in-law was working in my department. That year, my uncle and aunt decided to make a trip to the old country. This was my uncle's first time going back since he left his home back in his twenties.

In April of 1961, they sailed on the *Queen Mary* ship to spend six months in Europe. During that time, in addition to my work and social life, I also had to take care of the house. My uncle's friend had a summerhouse outside the city, and occasionally, he would ask me to spend the weekend there and help him with some carpentry work in the renovation of the house. On one of those trips, I met a friend of the family, a Croatian girl named Joan. She was good-looking and very smart. Joan did not speak Serbo-Croatian, but it did not matter to me since I spoke English relatively well. We spent much of our free time together and mostly went to the movies. As time went by, things got heated up, and she was falling in love with me, and she wanted to get married. This was not something that I was looking for at this time of my life, even though I liked Joan very much. I tried to defuse the situation, in fact, to break up our relationship, but it did not go very well with her. At that time, I realized that I was in a serious situation because my dream after I became a citizen of the United States was to go back to Montenegro and get married there. Vera, the girl from my childhood, was still on my mind, even though we had no communication at that time.

My uncle and aunt had just returned from Europe, and I did not have enough courage to tell them about the situation I was in with Joan. One day, while I was at work, Joan's relative, without her knowledge, came to visit my uncle and aunt to talk to them about Joan, being very emotional and heartbroken. This lady expressed great concern about Joan's emotional state, fearing what may happen to her if we do not get married. Of course, my folks did not know any of this. They thanked the lady for coming and told her that they would speak with me about this situation. Sure enough, when I got home from work, I was faced with questions about Joan and the situation I was in. I told my uncle and aunt that I liked Joan very much, but I had no intention of getting married at this time. Instead, I would like to speed up my draft to join the army. It seemed to me the decision I made was the best way out of this situation. In a few days, I went to the army recruiting station to inquire about joining the army. Since I was already a candidate for enlistment, they gave me the form to fill out to speed up my draft, which I did right there and then. Shortly after my draft inquiry, I was notified to report for physical examination at Whitehall Army Recruiting Station in downtown Manhattan. I passed the examination with flying colors, and now I was awaiting orders when to report for duty. At work, there was no problem with leaving the company because they had a policy for anyone going to serve the country could return to the same work position that was held prior to leaving.

A few weeks later, I received the orders to report for duty on February 9, 1962. I was processed and then transported to the basic training camp at Fort Dix, New Jersey. This was just two years since my arrival from the old country, and now I was sworn into the Armed Forces of the United States. Considering the circumstances of the past, my emotions were very high, and the feelings were great. I felt proud and eager to face the challenges coming ahead. I arrived at Fort Dix with many other recruits from the New York City area, and immediately, we were taken to the orientation station for the unit assignment, followed by the trip to the Quartermaster building to be issued the uniforms, boots, and all other necessary clothing. Also, we were assigned an M-1 rifle with complete gear. From now on, as the drill sergeant said, "You are not authorized to think. Instead, you will do as you are told." I fully understood and accepted the meaning of this statement, which made my life in the coming days and months much easier to cope with. The next morning at six, while still asleep, the drill sergeant came to our barrack as a madman, yelling from the top of his lungs, "First call! Reveille! Get up! Get out!" and so on. Being that this was the first morning, no one expected this wild outburst. We got dressed in a hurry and lined up in front of our barrack. The sergeant performed a roll call by calling our names, and we had to reply loudly, "Here!" or "Present!" Then he dismissed us for breakfast and to get ready for daily activities. This activity was repeated every morning after, but after a while, we got used to it. The sergeant was mean all the time, but that was the act he was putting on to make us or break us, or as he put it, "separate the men from the boys." The training program was mainly designed for physical conditioning, familiarization, and the use of basic weapons. Every day, we had a grueling schedule, so at the end of each day, we were so exhausted that we could not think of anything else but sleep. The army life started setting in, and I felt the decision I made to join the army was the right one. It got me away from my problems in my love life, which got me into a predicament that I did not know how to handle. The army gave me a chance to sort out my priorities, in other words, to hit the reset button and start over. After several weeks of training, I was in excellent physical condition, which helped me achieve excellent results in going through different faces of training. In addition to physical training, now we started going to the rifle range for the target practice. This was something that I enjoyed very much, and it did not take very long to show my skills in sharpshooting on a rifle range. Shortly after, on my first competition for excellent rifle shooting, I was awarded the "Army Rifle Expert Badge," which I wore proudly on my uniform. The spring of 1962 was approaching rapidly, and the weather was warming up, but the best news of all was that we were getting close to the end of our basic training. The end of the training was marked with a large military parade, and we were given the certificate of completion and one week of vacation, along with the orders to report back for an additional two months of advanced training.

For my vacation, I returned back home to my folks to have much-needed rest and relaxation. I had lots of stories to tell, as I really went through a grueling schedule of training. These vivid memories of the basic training will stay with me for the rest of my life. Considering the problems I had with my girlfriend Joan prior to enlisting in the army, I made a wise decision not to contact her or any other girlfriend from the past. The week of vacation went fast, and I was on my way back to Fort Dix, New Jersey, for two more months of advanced training. When I reported back for duty, I was assigned to a company for training with heavy weapons (for infantry support MOS 112.10). This time around, the conditions were improved somewhat, but we still had to go through lots of physical training, as well as the classroom instructions and the firing range for each of the heavy weapons. Not surprisingly, I enjoyed being around these weapons. I started training with an M60 machine gun, then a 50-caliber machine gun, followed by 81 mm mortar, 4.2-inch mortar, and 106 mm recoilless gun. Of all the weapons, I liked the 106 mm recoilless gun because, at that time, it was the best tactical anti-tank weapon mounted on the jeep for rapid deployment. This weapon was equipped with a 50-caliber machine gun mounted on the top. The machine gun would be used to mark the target by firing one round of white phosphorus bullets, and if it lands on the target, immediately squeeze the trigger of the big gun. In addition to practicing on all firing ranges, we had to learn how to assemble and disassemble all types of weapons, where we had many competitions for speed and accuracy. Also, cleaning the weapons was very important. Every Saturday was dedicated to all types of inspections, starting with personal hygiene, then living quarters such as bunk beds, footlockers with the booths on display, and all other personal belongings. The bed had to be made up, the blanket folded straight and tight, so the sergeant would throw the coin in the middle of the bed, and if the coin bounced, it would be fine, but if it did not, he would pull the blanket, and it had to be made over. In addition to training, all other activities, such as inspections, guard duties, kitchen work, parades, etc., were designed to keep the troops occupied at all times. By now, we were highly trained on all the weapons at our disposal and ready for deployment to face any situation that may come our way.

These were very unsettled times, in the middle of the Cold War, between the Soviet Union and the United States with allies. In our hemisphere, the Cuban missile crisis was brewing. In Asia, the Vietnam War was raging on, and in Europe, mainly Germany, the large presence of troops had to be maintained due to the tensions with the Soviet Union. After the completion of my advanced training, I was given one week of leave and ordered to report back for the next assignment to the Third Armored Division, which was stationed in Germany. After my leave of absence, I returned to Fort Dix, where I was processed and transported to Fort Hamilton, New York, to board the transport ship USNS *General Alexander Patch*. This was a large ship and no comparison to the ship *Vulcania* that I came on from Europe. Boarding the ship took some time because of the large size of troops and its complexity, but finally, we were ordered to assemble in formation on the top decks of the ship. On the pier was positioned the large military band. Over the ship's speakers came loud orders, calling for attention and salute, while the band was playing the national anthem. This was one of the finest moments that I have ever experienced, with feelings that came over me, full of pride, accomplishment, and readiness to defend and protect the United States of America. The commanding officer stressed the importance of our difficult mission and reminded us that we are all the ambassadors of the United States and that we should represent our country in the best way possible. This was a very powerful and emotional send-off on a long voyage of many days to the port of Bremerhaven, Germany. We sailed in the evening into the darkness of the Atlantic Ocean, and then we settled down for the standard rules and regulations of the ship's captain. The days were long, and not much to do, but we tried to cope with the situation as best we could. There was a chance to occasionally see the movie, which was also good to pass the time. Periodically, during the day, we would see a periscope of the submarine in proximity to the ship and sometimes would even surface on the water. Suppose that was our escort and, perhaps, the insurance policy to protect us from the unknown. The daily bulletin with a lot of news, weather, and sports was available to us so we could follow what was going on back home and abroad. I enjoyed reading and never missed an issue, but from what I could see, not many soldiers cared about most of that information, other than some sports. This was the beginning of summer when the weather was nice and the ocean rather calm, so we had it made. It seemed the ship was in no hurry, as it was moving rather slowly, which gave us an indication that there was a ship schedule, when to arrive in port of Bremerhaven. The ship traffic was steadily increasing as we were approaching the English Channel on the way north to Bremerhaven, which is in the northern part of Germany. The ship was carrying many soldiers for different army bases in Germany, so on arrival, we were assigned to the groups accordingly. Disembarking the ship was a lengthy process, followed by transport to the train to take us south to Gelnhausen, about thirty miles away from Frankfurt am Main. This was an overnight ride, so we arrived in Gelnhausen in the morning, where the army trucks were waiting to take us to the military base nearby. I was assigned to the Third Armored Division, Forty-eighth Infantry, Second Battalion, Company "C," Fourth platoon / heavy weapons. Approaching the main gate to the base was already impressive enough, then riding on the main street, lining up on both sides with large buildings, and finally stopping in front of Company "C." We were told to report to the officer on duty for processing. For the next eighteen months, this was my new home, so it was entirely up to me to determine what level of success I could accomplish. One of the first and most important topics that I had to absorb was the importance of emergency drills, so-called "alerts." The entire base was equipped with sirens that could sound off at any time, day or night. When the siren came on, everyone was required to report to their unit and the proper vehicle that they were assigned to for immediate evacuation of the base. These alerts were at the total discretion of the commanding officer, who would call it off sometime shortly after it sounded off, but other times, he would order full-field maneuvers for many days and many miles away from the home base. When this happens, the entire Third Armored Division, with all its might, would be on the move, choking up the roads and towns on the way. This was designed to boost the readiness of the troops in case of an enemy attack. The troop movement of this magnitude could not be done without a great extent of damage to the communities subjected to the military maneuvers.

The United States government would send its adjusters to appraise the damage done by the Army maneuvers and compensate the German authorities for the restoration. This was the regular army, and the life here on the base was much more different than in the basic training. From the first call/reveille at 6:00 a.m. to 5:00 p.m. was a regular working day unless you were on a special assignment beyond the normal duty hours. After working hours, it was possible to request a special pass to go to the town, but you had to be back before the midnight curfew.

From the beginning, the mess hall and the kitchen were staffed by German civilian workers, but later, due to security concerns, the change was made, and the soldiers had to take over this additional duty. No matter what my assignment was, it seemed that nothing was hard for me to do, and I was adjusting nicely to those new surroundings and even made some close friends. About three weeks after my arrival in Germany, sometime in the evening hours, the sirens went on, and the alert was officially on. At that time, I happened to be in the building, where I immediately grabbed the duffle bag and the rifle with complete gear and ran across the field to my designated APC (armored personnel carrier) to join the rest of my platoon. In less than five minutes, the engine was on, and we were ready to roll in the column for the total evacuation from the base. This was something that I had never experienced before; the entire Third Armored Division was on the move into the darkness of the night for a destination that only commanders knew. In the dawn hours of the morning, we ended up near the town of Fulda, some fifty miles away from the base. Upon the arrival, the sergeant in charge started immediately assigning everyone's position with specific duties. I was assigned to guard duty on the intersection of the country road and the afoot trail.

The surroundings were mainly flat terrain with very little vegetation, where the rest of my platoon was spread around guarding various positions. Standing on a dirt road in the middle of nowhere did not make much sense to me, but that did not matter what I thought. It had to be obeyed.

Not even fifteen minutes on my guard duty when I heard the sound of the helicopter above, coming closer and closer, just to land about thirty yards away from me. I was new to this kind of situation to be in, and it made me worried about why the helicopter was landing close to my position. Upon landing, Major Joel J. Williams stepped out of the helicopter and walked straight toward my position, which made me think fast about what to do in this situation. As Major Williams came closer, I drew my weapon and shouted, "Halt!" He stopped and identified himself, then walked closer to me and told me to "At ease, Private." He read my name from the fatigues uniform and then asked me softly where I came from. When I told him that

I came from Yugoslavia, he continued with more questions about how long I was in the States and asked me about my education. The final question was "Franovich, would you like to attend the school at the base?" My answer was loud and clear, "Yes, sir," then he said, "See me when we return to the home base." I followed with the salute and "Thank you, sir." Major Williams returned to the helicopter and flew away. At that time, I could not believe what had just happened to me. Was I imagining that, or did it really happen? Now I truly believe being in the right place at the right time is what everyone needs, at least once in a lifetime. Back in Yugoslavia, I completed elementary and middle school in addition to two and a half years of trade school. Since I did not attend any high school in the States, it would mean that, upon completion, I could only receive the high school equivalency diploma, but even that would open the door for the further education that I wanted so much. The Third Armored Division, which I was part of, had a complete education center on the base, staffed with professional teachers from the States to help many soldiers complete their high school education.

Those maneuvers lasted for ten days and were designed as a part of large-scale training, not only for the general troops but also for high-ranking officers. We were bivouacking in the field and slept in the army tents (shelter half), which we carried with us as a part of the individual gear. Every company would be followed by a supply convoy consisting of a mess truck, special trucks that were equipped with field latrines, showers, fuel, and the field ambulance. Considering my growing up in a house with no basic services such as electricity and running water until I was fifteen years old, these field conditions that I was experiencing looked very good to me, especially getting hot meals and showers in the field.

Every day, sometimes even at night, we were given orders for different missions to attack or defend certain positions. My platoon had responsibility for the infantry support with heavy weapons (mortars), and we fired life ammunition. I was trained to operate the M16 plotting board, the instrument to calculate the information for the gunsights, so they can accurately fire on the targets. The forward observer is the person who goes ahead of the infantry to spot the enemy targets and then reports that information over the radio. When I receive the enemy position, longitude, and latitude, I calculate the information (elevation and deflection) for the gunsights for accurate firing on the enemy position.

We were getting very good at that, no surprise. After all, we had all that training. It required the teamwork to be the best we could be.

When the division commanding officer called the field exercise off, the orders came down to our company commander to follow the sequence of engagement to a column formation and to proceed orderly return to the base.

The vehicles we were riding on were the APCs, equipped with tracks, the same as the tanks, and the speed and maneuverability were limited. It took us a whole day to cover some fifty miles. Finally, after ten days of living in the woods, we were happy to take a hot shower and enjoy a warm meal. Even so, we were back, but our job related to the field maneuvers was not over yet, as we had to pull maintenance on the vehicles and equipment. For a few days following the field trip, the daily schedule was lighter than usual to give us a chance to relax for a while. The most favorable place on the whole base was the NCO (noncommissioned officers) club, where the soldiers would gather and, in most cases, spend the last dime. Some soldiers would spend more money than they would receive from the monthly pay, so they had to borrow money from their friends and, in some cases, even pay the interest on the borrowed money. At that time, my rank was "private" with a monthly pay of $130, but with good management of money, it was sufficient for personal expenses and occasional get out to the town. A few days after our return from the field exercise, I gathered enough courage to visit Major Williams, as he instructed me during our encounter in the field. Normally, I would have to seek permission from my company sergeant to see Major Williams, but in this case, he told me to visit him upon our return from the field trip, so I went directly to his office. Major Williams remembered me very well, but he wanted to know more about my background. Perhaps he wanted to be fully convinced that I really wanted to attend the school. Finally, he wrote a letter and told me to take it to the officer in charge of the education center.

In the letter were the instructions for the officer in charge of the education center to enroll me in the program and to excuse me from all duties except for the emergency drills and alerts. I had to wait a few weeks until school started. In the meantime, I was asserting myself well in the position that I was in. The corporals and the sergeants were very good at what they were doing, but beyond that, lacked education and, most importantly, did not have much common sense. I knew how they were operating, so I always tried to be one step ahead of them, not to be subjected to their inability for a rational reason. During this period of waiting for my school to begin, I was notified that I was promoted to the private first class, so with the stripe on my sleeve came a little more money and some privileges. We were often going to practice firing heavy weapons, also in between small arms. My scoring records from the firing ranges were all excellent, sharpshooter or expert, which earned me a lot of respect all the way to the company commander.

At the base, we had a movie theater with frequent changes of new films and a library where we could spend some free time or check out books of interest. The librarian's name was Renata, the young German girl, and in time, we became very good friends. So I was even invited to her home, where I met her parents. In the days ahead, there will be more details on this relationship. Two years before my arrival at the Third Armored Division, the most well-known name, Elvis Presley, was also serving at this same base. During World War II, General George S. Patton spearheaded this famous division deep into the heart of Germany, capturing ten thosuand square miles of enemy territory in just ten days. My arrival to the Third Army did not make any difference, but it did make me personally proud to be part of this unit that was second to none and always at a combat-ready status.

The days were marching on, and it was almost time for my school to start. My company commander was notified of me attending the school, which excused me from all other duties, and I was ready to go.

To be placed in the proper grade level, I was subjected to a series of tests in all subjects and was assigned books accordingly. At first, I was a little nervous, but overall scoring went very well, and now I became officially a student at the US Armed Forces Institute–European Division. I felt like the luckiest person in the world, and all that was attributed to Major Williams for his unforgettable recommendation for my further education. I took my school very seriously because I knew that, for me, this was once in a lifetime opportunity to complete these required courses to pursue higher education. Most of my study was done at the library, where I could concentrate and do my home assignments. One pleasant distraction was only Renata, the librarian, who was intensely studying me and every move I made. I was a soldier, so I did not mind some attention; in fact, I was encouraging that, and before long, we became very good friends. I was very much aware of my complicated relationship with a girl, Joan in New York, that landed me in the army before I needed to, so I tried to strike a balance between romantic involvement and a good friendship. In most situations, this is an almost impossible task, but fortunately for me, this kind of relationship worked for a good while. Renata was a very smart girl and fun to be with. She would invite me to her house for lunch and to be with her parents. Her father and I did not get along very well, mainly because he was a German soldier in Yugoslavia during World War II. On one occasion, he told me that Yugoslav partisans did not respect the Geneva Convention Treaty (rules of war), as they were fired upon while parachuting during the attack on Yugoslavia. That was hard for me to swallow, and calmly, I replied, "What were you doing there?" He also did not like Americans, so my uniform did not sit well with him. From time to time, we exchanged digs at each other, but I tried to stay away from him. Through a mutual friend, I met a fellow soldier named John, who was born in Dalmatia, Yugoslavia, and spoke my language, so we had many things in common. John was married, and his wife, Suzanne, and son were in California while he was trying to bring them to Germany. It did not take very long before Suzanne, with her baby boy, joined John, so he rented an apartment for them near the base. We became very good friends, so good that they asked me to be the godfather to baby John Jr. at his baptism. Renata and I were frequent guests of John and Suzanne, and we enjoyed many delicious meals they would prepare. John introduced me to his friend Tony, who was American-born with roots in Croatia and Yugoslavia, and we, too, became very good friends. Occasionally, on weekends, we would altogether make a trip to Frankfurt by train, which is twenty-nine kilometers from our army base. Frankfurt had many attractions to visit and spend a day, but most of all was great to be away from the army base. Looking back on those days, I do not know how I managed to balance my extra curriculum of study with social activity and remain the good soldier that I was. Despite all the activity that I was surrounded with, my mind was wandering all over, from my folks and the job in New York to Vera and the relatives in Yugoslavia. While I was in Germany, I did not have any contact with Vera or anyone else in Yugoslavia, but they were on my mind all the time. My feelings for Vera were with me all the time, but it felt like I had put her in a time capsule to reactivate her later. If I could relive those days, certainly Vera would be at the forefront of my life. In school, I was doing exceptionally well in all the subjects, but mathematics was my favorite from the very beginning. My hope was if I completed high school successfully, I'd continue my education upon returning to civilian life. I knew that was a big wish to hope for, but I was a strong believer in positive thinking. Later, I even read a book called *The Power of Positive Thinking*. So from the early days of my life, my mind was set on the right path to march forward and never look back. Many soldiers around me were not adjusting well to the army way of life, and many times, they were getting singled out for their behavior. Complaints and resisting orders from their superiors would earn them extra guard duty or (KP) kitchen work. On October 5, 1962, we were honored by the visit of the Secretary of Defense Robert S. McNamara to the Third Armored Division. Following his visit to our unit, we were engaged in another large field exercise.

Testing speed, mobility, and striking power, the Third Armored Division wound up the active year by moving to the field with other units for FTX sabre knot. The exercise involved more than thirty thousand troops, and it was conducted in below-zero temperatures. These troop movements were the large war games to build up conditions and the skills needed to achieve good results if ever needed on the battlefield.

The time was moving on fast, and my school study was progressing well despite interruptions by the large field maneuvers. Another big event was underway in preparation for the visit of President John F. Kennedy to West Germany. This was a historical visit by the president of the United States in support of the West German government during the peak of the Cold War. On June 25, 1963, in the field of Hanau, Germany, we assembled over fifteen thousand troops with every weapon in the arsenal that we had, including tactical nuclear weapons, for the president's review. I was very proud to be part of this historic day, and I was anxiously awaiting the president to arrive. Our company commander pulled several arms inspections to make sure that our weapons were clear of ammunition. Finally, the large convertible limousine was approaching, with President Kennedy sitting behind the driver and to his right, accompanied by Major General John R. Pugh, commanding general of the Third Armored Division of which I was a member. I was positioned in the front row of Company "C," Forty-Eighth Infantry, in the perfect view of the president. As the car was approaching some fifteen feet in front of me, the company commander called us to attention that followed with the salute, while the president was riding by. When he spoke to the troops, he stated that it was one of the finest military formations he had ever seen. It was a spectacular display of force that will live in my memory forever.

While the president had lunch with the noncommissioned officers, the troops had one of the best barbecue stakes in the field. The army grills were very simple, made from fifty-five-gallon drums, split in half, and covered with heavy gauge mesh wire. The next day, June 26, 1963,

President Kennedy arrived in Berlin and was greeted by the chancellor of the Federal Republic of Germany, Konrad Adenauer, and the mayor of West Berlin, Willy Brandt. The president delivered his famous speech to the citizens of Berlin with his unforgettable words, "Ich bin ein Berliner." It seemed to me that there was no shortage of major events in those days, and in some way, all those activities affected my social life.

Shortly after the president's visit, on July 23, 1963, there was a major earthquake in the Yugoslav city of Skopje, with over a thousand deaths and many more injured. The Third Armored Division was sending aid of food, blankets, equipment, and teams of rescuers in search of the survivors. Since I spoke the language, I wanted to go as the interpreter, but I was nearing the finals in the school, so I could not go. So after all these past activities, I returned to my heavy focus on my study. The challenge was serious, but I performed very well, and the results of my final examinations were excellent. I scored high in all the subjects, which qualified me to receive the high school equivalency diploma from the State of New York. With this achievement, I laid the groundwork for the continuation of my further education when I return to civilian life. Now that I finished school, I returned to my duty of full daily schedule. The company commander and the sergeant congratulated me on my achievement in the school.

As the older soldiers were nearing discharge, the new troops were coming from the states as the replacements. The seniority in the army and the higher rank played a very important part in the scheduling of the work duty, so the newcomers always ended up with most of the work. Shortly after my school completion, I was promoted to a Specialist fourth class, which gave me an increase in pay and more authority. With my extra pay, I was purchasing US saving bonds to help me financially when I returned to civilian life. The closer I got to my discharge, the more thoughts were coming to my mind regarding my job, applying for citizenship, continuing my education, and making a trip to my homeland that by now I missed very much. During this time, our daily activities include a lot of classroom instructions on weapons and personal survival. Frequently, we had to practice going through the gas chamber (tear gas) as part of training. It consisted of entering the chamber, placing over the face a gas mask, and then saying the name, rank, and serial number before exiting. This training was designed to gain confidence in handling gas masks in case of dangerous enemy gas attacks. We all hated this process very much, but it had to be done.

With everything going normally and being least expected, the sirens sounded alert, and once again, the entire Third Armored Division was on the move. This was called the operation "Big Lift." It began on October 30, 1963, and lasted for seven days. Our division acted as aggressor for the Second Armored Division airlifted from Fort Hood, Texas, with action as "enemy" forces.

The Third Armored Division lived up to its reputation and achieved excellent results. Once again, it felt good to be part of these historic war games designed to show the world the strength and capabilities of the United States forces. On the return to the base, after seven days of grueling field exercise, we were exhausted but still had to go through the standard procedure of pulling maintenance on weapons and equipment. After every large maneuver like this one, life on the base would return to some normality, where we could receive the pass to visit nearby towns for some entertainment and relaxation with friends.

On Friday, November 22, 1963, in the evening hours, we were called for formation in the front of our building. I knew something big was happening as this kind of activity was never done before. Everyone around me had the same feelings. We thought, perhaps, the war broke out. Finally, the company commander arrived and called us to attention. There was a slight tremble in his voice, and he spoke softly, announcing that the president of the United States, John F. Kennedy, was shot to death in Dallas, Texas. He further stated that until further notice, all leaves were canceled, all passes were suspended, and no one was allowed to leave the base for any reason. It felt as if the ground sunk under our feet, some unforgettable sight. It was absolute silence. Some soldiers even started crying. The next morning, the flag was flown at half-staff and continued for the next thirty days. The main gates of our base were open to the German citizens for the mass to be conducted on the football field at the base. From the building of my Company "C," I could see the German people pouring in and quickly filling the field. Some information was coming in slowly, but largely, we were uninformed as everyone was extremely anxious to find out what was happening back home. These were extremely difficult times for the country but especially dangerous times for the soldiers on the front line. The Cold War was raging on, and any incident could spark a disaster for the world. That is why troop movement of any kind was restricted indefinitely. The president's visit to our troops last June was still fresh in our minds, and we could not believe what happened to our commander in chief. My life, in these trying times, was full of sorrow and uncertainty with a lot of worry about what may happen in the future. Coming from the war-torn country of Yugoslavia, where I lost so much, I was fully aware of the dangers we were facing at those difficult times, especially in this part of the world, where the United States had a presence of over 360,000 US troops. Slowly, we were returning to normality, where we started resuming training and everyday activities. The time of my tour duty in Germany was coming close to an end, so I was faced with the campaign for the reenlistment. There was a reenlisting committee working on every soldier to reenlist for three more years. In my situation, considering my rank and education, I was offered the rank of sergeant (E-5), a bonus of three thousand dollars in cash, and enrollment in the helicopter flying school. In those days, the United States was heavily involved in the Vietnam War, where there was a shortage of helicopter pilots, so there was an urgent need to recruit new candidates for the pilot school. Considering the danger of this mission if I accepted the offer and my ambition to seek opportunities in civilian life, I declined the offer made to me by the reenlisting officer. There was a military regulation that applied to every soldier to obtain clearance from every contact on the base prior to leaving for the United States. Some of those places were laundry and dry cleaning, library, service club, post office, army PX, etc. The last clearance was to turn in the weapon and the personal gear. This was to make sure that the soldiers settled all accounts on the base and did not have something in their possession that belonged to someone else before leaving.

Finally, I received my clearance papers, and I had ten days to visit all the contacts and have it certified that I did not owe anything to anyone. This was one of the easiest times since I entered the army. Part of this going around the base was also used to visit friends and say goodbye with the hope to meet again someday in civilian life. In fact, I stayed in touch with John, Tony, and Arpad to this very day, nearing sixty years since that time. With all that excitement of going home, there was also some sadness of leaving. Since my arrival in Germany, in the last eighteen months, many things have happened, and many friends have been made, which have changed my life in many ways. The final day of my tour duty in Germany had arrived, and I joined many other soldiers to be transported overnight to Bremerhaven, where the ship was awaiting the arrival of the troops from many different locations around the country. *General William O. Darby*, the Navy transport ship, was servicing the rotation of the US troops in the capacity of carrying 1,307 soldiers. Our destination port was Ft. Hamilton, New York City, to be discharged from the army. This time of the year, sailing in the Atlantic Ocean was rough, and we had tough going for many days. I was on my third time crossing the Atlantic, so I knew what to expect and how to cope with that situation. Many times, some soldiers did not show up for the meals, as the seasickness was taking over. The daily bulletin was available to us, with some news and the weather. One day, the word came out that the ship had to slow down and wait for the orders to suit the port schedule. Finally, in the morning hours of January 27, 1964, our ship docked in the port. Once again, we were lined up in formation, the national anthem played, and the commanding officer gave the welcoming speech for our return to the United States with the service well done. Following the orderly process, we disembarked from the ship and were issued so-called form 214 for the completion of the two years of active duty. My military status for the next two years was active reserve, meaning that I could be called to serve two weeks reserve at any time during that period, and the last two years were inactive reserve, which meant I could be only called to serve in case of a national emergency. The total army service obligation was six years, at the end of which would be issued the final discharge.

These were happy times for me, as I was proudly entering civilian life, once again, with a long list of accomplishments for the past two years. My folks were equally happy to see me back home. On my return, I took two weeks of vacation for some rest and relaxation before returning to my old job at the Stimpson Company. One of the first things I had to do was pull maintenance on my car, which was stored in the garage for the past two years. The cars those days could be easily repaired, and I was doing most of the work myself. My two weeks of vacation were short, but it gave me enough time to get some rest and to reflect in time where I have been and what I have done. By any imagination, it was a remarkable achievement that I accomplished in the military service, which made me proud, and I was anxious to return to work and share my experiences with fellow workers. On my first day back to work, I was welcomed back by the foreman and the supervisor as well as all others that I worked with before going to the army. I can say it felt great to be back, and I was already looking for opportunities for advancement in this company. The late department where I was working was on the second floor, adjacent to the engineering and drafting, with a partial glass partition. I started eyeing that department, and every day forward, something was coming over me, urging me to inquire about the requirements it would take to be transferred into that department.

One day, I gathered enough courage to approach my foreman with an inquiry about transferring into the drafting department and further explained that I had completed my high school education in the army, loved sketching, and mathematics was my favorite subject. The foreman was very nice and told me that he was going to speak with the supervisor. His answer alone was very encouraging enough to raise my hopes of getting ahead. The Stimpson Company was known for its practices of promoting within and giving opportunities for advancement. A few days later, the supervisor called me into his office and started explaining to me that for someone to be considered for the position in the drafting department, he would have to at least have some drafting skills to have the position open. He suggested that if I was that determined, I needed to sign up for drafting class in the evening school, and if I showed good results, they would take that under consideration. That was music to my ears and all I wanted to hear.

Immediately, I started searching for schools offering courses in drafting. The Mechanic Institute at Forty-Fourth Street in New York City was offering a three-year program in mechanical drafting, just what I was looking for. Being that I lived in the borough of Queens, worked in Brooklyn, and for the next three years, going to school in Manhattan was a bit of a challenge, but I was so determined that nothing could get in my way. I enrolled in the school that was going to start in September of 1964. During that summer, in the city of New York was a social unrest, with devastating race-related riots that started in Harlem, upper Manhattan. These riots were spreading fast to Brooklyn and Jamaica, Queens, and many other places, mostly in African American neighborhoods. This violent and dangerous situation was also sweeping many cities across the country, and everyone was living on the edge. I was personally exposed to danger every day of the week by walking to and from work. Going to work, I was using the subway, where I would get off at the Flushing station in Brooklyn, then walk by the city housing project, fearing danger from falling objects, as the youngsters were throwing bricks from the top of buildings, causing fear among pedestrians. During this difficult time of disorder, riots, and destruction of property, the mayor of NYC was Robert F. Wagner, a Democrat. At work, most of our conversations were related to the problems in the city and across the country. It was those days when I started leaning toward the Republican Party, as their philosophy was coinciding with my line of thinking. I could not vote yet, but I was anxiously awaiting my fifth anniversary in the United States, when I would be eligible to apply for US citizenship.

During that summer, while waiting for the school to start in September, in addition to my regular job, I was working on the weekends, a part-time job at the gas station close to LaGuardia Airport. The owner of that gas station had a contract with the car rental companies at the airport to fuel and service all vehicles. When a customer returned the rental car to the airport, my job was to go there, pick up that car, drive it to the gas station to be washed, fill it with gas, and return back to the airport. This sounds very easy to do, but on the contrary, it was a very demanding and exhausting job. The rental cars were new, and some of them were convertible, which gave me the pleasure of driving those cars at higher speeds. This was also the year when the Beatles came to America, when Beatlemania magic occupied the minds and hearts of young people. I was one of those people, and my portable radio was working overtime too. Working so many hours per week did not leave any time for social life, but my goal was to save some money and make a trip next year to Yugoslavia. Finally, the time came for me to start the school. My class on mechanical drafting was held on the third floor of the Mechanics Institute. The first day of school was mostly for the orientation and purchase of school supplies needed for the class, which were available at the school supply store located on the first floor. That same day, we were also assigned to a drafting table to be used for the rest of the school year. There were twenty-two students in my class, with a mix of many different backgrounds and nationalities. Next to my table was a fellow student named Edward Juchniewicz, a Polish immigrant whom I called Edy. I don't know how or why, but from the first moment of our meeting, we formed a bond of friendship that extended far beyond our school days and included our families to be inseparable ever since. I will have much more on our friendship throughout the years. Our drafting class instructor started teaching us how to develop basic skills, how to draw a line, that is object line, dimension line, etc. To draw a proper line, the pencil hardness played a very important part, so all these basics were necessary to produce quality drawings.

At the very beginning of every drawing, it is most important to select the proper type of paper to be used to have quality reproduction, that is to make a copy through the blueprint machine. We were systematically introduced to drawing geometric shapes, then solid objects, followed by two and three views of an object, and so on. I was eager to learn as my sight was set on the drafting department in my company, but more than that, I got to enjoy the school. My friend Edy and I were getting our work done much faster and accurately than the rest of the class, and the instructor took notice of that by presenting our work as an example to the class. Usually Fridays after school, Edy and I would go for a coffee, where we would tell each other stories of our lives and coming to America. At the time, Edy was married to a German lady who was working as a secretary to one major TV Network. He was telling me of all the difficulties he had in his marriage, as his wife wanted to return to Germany, which he hated. He remembered the days when the German Army invaded Poland in World War II, and the Soviet Union annexed the east part of the country where his family was living. Many Polish citizens were transported to labor camps throughout Siberia, and Edy, as a small child, was among those families. When he was describing what he went through, I could see his eyes were tearing. I thought my childhood was difficult until I heard Edy's story of growing up in Siberia and what he went through in coming to America. The repatriation of Polish citizens from the Soviet Union started after the pact was signed in November 1956 between Poland and the Soviet Union. Finally, Edy returned to Poland just to find another Communist regime, with no chance to emigrate to the United States. He found a job to work as a crane operator on a loading dock at the sea port of Gdansk, loading the ships with various materials. From the first day on the job, he was planning the escape from Poland to anywhere in the West. One night, somehow using the crane and some cable, he managed to lower himself to the top deck of the ship, where he was hiding under some electrical transformers. Sailing through the Baltic Sea in the winter, on the outside open deck, could be deadly. The ship was going to Sweden, and on arrival there, he was discovered nearly frozen. At last, he was a freeman, and with the help of the American embassy, he eventually got to the United States.

In January of 1965, five years after my arrival in the United States, I was eligible, and immediately, I applied for citizenship. A month or so later, I had an appointment with the immigration and naturalization service for an oral and written test. The examiner was very friendly and started telling me that the past weekend, he had dinner with Ex-King Peter of Yugoslavia. I grew up in Yugoslavia, a communist country, and the only thing I learned in school about the king was that in 1941, during World War II, he abandoned the country and its people for exile in London, and in later years, he was some sort of salesman. I sensed that the examiner was a good friend of Ex-King Peter, and I did not know where he was going with his story, so I chose not to say anything. He continued by asking me many questions about the US presidents, the Constitution, and my service in the army. He complimented me on my good answers and told me that upon the review, I would be notified when to appear for swearing-in ceremony. Some weeks later, in a group of a few hundred applicants, I was sworn in as a citizen of the United States. For the past five years since my arrival to the States, I had many accomplishments, but becoming a citizen was one of the achievements that made me most proud. Everything was progressing smoothly as if I had planned every step of the way, and shortly after, I obtained a US passport with the plan for July to make a vacation trip to Yugoslavia. The excitement was already building up, and my mind was going in many different directions, from the schoolwork to my job at Stimpson, to my friends, and now new planning of a vacation trip, with a big prospect of getting married. My uncle Steve and aunt Maria were also planning to spend the summer in Yugoslavia, and they knew that I would join them for a short time, but they did not know of my intentions to get married during my trip.

The Stimpson Company was closing for vacation, the first two weeks of July every year, so I arranged to take another week of leave to have enough time to accomplish my plans. In the meantime, I received a notice from the army to report for the active reserve, the last two weeks of August in Fort Drum, upstate New York. This was something that I did not need at that time, but there was no way around that except just following the orders.

Fortunately, the call for the army reserve was not interfering with my vacation or the beginning of the next school year in September, so I could move forward with my plans.

I purchased my airline ticket on TWA to London from London to Belgrade, and on to Podgorica, Montenegro, on (JAT) Yugoslav airline. This was my first trip to be flying across the Atlantic Ocean, so I was looking forward to that. My uncle and aunt had already left for Yugoslavia, and my school year just ended, so I had more personal time to get ready for my trip. At my job at Stimpson Company, I was gaining seniority, and by then, I was able to operate any machine in the department just because the foreman was giving me more complex tool orders that required the use of different equipment. The day before vacation, we spent the entire day cleaning and servicing the machines and equipment so everything would be in the best working condition upon our return from vacation.

The day had come, the suitcase was packed, and I was on my way to Kennedy Airport. Instead of being very happy, some anxiety took over me for not knowing how all this was going to play out. I was feeling guilty that for the past five and a half years, I did not communicate much with anyone, especially with Vera. I realized, during that time, many things happened to me, and I was very busy, but still, that was only an excuse. I knew Vera was in college, and I was most certain that she had a lot of friends, perhaps a boyfriend that she cared for very much. All these thoughts were going through my mind while riding in the cab to the airport. Getting on the airplane went smoothly, and I was under way on the first leg of my trip. This was an overnight flight, getting in London morning hours, then I had to transfer to the Yugoslav Airline gate and wait for its departure. As I was waiting there, the most people, if not all, gathering at the gate were Yugoslav passengers. Most of them were smoking, and you could see blue-white smoke filling the room. I was not a smoker, so this much smoke did not sit well with me, but I could not do anything about that situation, as it was quite normal for them and permissible in those days. During the boarding, there were no seat assignments, so there was a lot of pushing and shoving to get on the plane, and finally, everyone settled down for two and a half hours of flying time to Belgrade. Followed by a thirty-minute flight to Podgorica, Montenegro, and sometime in the evening, I arrived in the village where I was born.

Upon my arrival, I was greeted by my relatives, and everyone was happy to see me, especially my aunt Milica, as I could see happy tears pouring down her face. I was emotional, too, but very happy to be back. After all, this is the place where I was born, with deep roots in everything I have done up to this point in my life. The trip was very long. That took about thirty hours to get there, and I was very tired, so right after dinner, I went to bed. Being away from the village life for all that time, I forgot how beautiful and tranquil it was, with all the greenfields filled with wildflowers and the birds singing in the morning. Not so much that I forgot, but before I left the village, I was much younger, so perhaps I did not appreciate as much all those beautiful surroundings. The next morning, my aunt Milica was briefing me on everyone in the village. I found out that my best friend Vladimir was in the army, his sister Vera was going to college in Dubrovnik, but she was home for the summer, and their parents built a house in

Petrovac. My first cousin Gojko and his family were living in Belgrade, but they came home to Petrovac for a summer vacation. Gojko and his sister Milena were older than me, but I enjoyed going to their house and staying overnight. Their mother, my aunt Katica, was always nice to me, and I liked her very much, so the very next day, upon my return there, I went to visit them. My next big move was to go to Vera's parents and test the waters with Vera. As I mentioned before while growing up in the village, I was spending lots of time in their house, and they always treated me as if I were one of their own children. Vladimir was my best friend, but perhaps Vera was the biggest reason that I was always around. When I got to their house, they were very happy to see me, and I got to see Vera again after five and a half years. I do not recall all the conversation between us, but as I was leaving, she said to me, "I will buy you a present to take with you back to America," and my reply was "I will take you instead, with me to America." Vera was always special to me, and now as I saw her again, she ignited my old feelings to the point that I was certain she was the one for me.

In that part of the world, in those days, it was customary that the man would choose a close family member to visit the parents of the girl to ask them for permission to marry their daughter and then seek the consent of the girl. I followed the customs in the region and asked my cousin Gojko and my uncle Steve to go to Vera's parents and ask them for the hand of their daughter. They were very happy to hear of my intention to get married, especially with someone they knew very well, so the next morning, they went to Vera's house to talk to her parents and then sought the final word from Vera. Her parents were overwhelmed with joy, but Vera was not at home. She was visiting her sister in the next town of Budva, some eighteen kilometers away from Petrovac. My cousin Gojko was not going to lose any time. He got into his car and drove to Budva to seek Vera's answer to my proposal. Vera said, "Yes," and Gojko brought her back home to her happy parents.

I had little more than two weeks left of my vacation, so we had to move very fast for the preparation of the wedding ceremony. Vera's brother Vladimir, who was at the time serving in the army, asked for an emergency leave to join us for the wedding, and all other relatives on Vera's and mine side were notified and invited. My best man was the son of my godparents, who was the town's doctor. We planned a civil marriage ceremony to be followed by dinner at my house in the village. With all those numerous events, Vera and I had very little time for ourselves. Our love for each other did not happen on the spur of the moment; rather, it was progressing from childhood. As I see it today, the word love is based on a feeling of emotions with some percent of risk attached to it, but true lifelong love is something of an entirely different proportion that must be maintained throughout life. My description of true love, in comparison, would be the closest to the school years, where, periodically, new subjects were added, and the tests had to be taken to continue. Behind that first physical love comes coping with children, facing financial burdens, understanding and compassion for each other, exhibiting respect, and being for each other in sickness and health. For any couple, a passing grade with high marks on all those tests throughout life would be a remarkable achievement of true love. At the time of our marriage, neither Vera nor I knew much of anything that was coming our way in the life ahead, but we committed ourselves to building our future around each other.

On July 18, 1965, with all our friends and guests, we gathered in the city hall in Petrovac, where the justice of peace officiated our wedding ceremony. Following the ceremony, we all went to our house in the village for dinner and festivity to the end of the day. This was very tiring for both of us, but finally, we were married, and that was all that mattered. We knew that Vera could not travel with me to the United States because there was not enough time to obtain a US entry visa for Vera, so the plan was that she would come later in the year with my uncle Steve and aunt Maria.

This time of the year in Montenegro is a great beach time, so we took advantage of that. We visited the beach, where we spent much of our free time together while growing up. I recalled a memory from those days when Vera was learning to swim. Of all the friends there, she was most comfortable with me and put her trust in me to help her. Perhaps all those little things between us at an early age were an expression of silent love. The end of my vacation was approaching rapidly, and we planned to go together to the American embassy in Belgrade to apply for Vera's visa to the United States. Then I would continue my trip back to New York while Vera returned home to wait for the visa. In Belgrade, we checked in the hotel not far from the

American embassy, so the next morning, we went there and submitted all the necessary documents with an application for Vera's entry visa. This was the last obligation that we had to do, and the next few days, we spent sightseeing and visiting some relatives who lived in Belgrade. Finally, the time had come for us to part away, but the good thing was that it was not for long. These were very difficult and emotional moments for both of us to say goodbye. As I was boarding the plane, I felt that a good part of me was left behind, and I was truly hurt. Vera went back to Montenegro to wait for the issuance of her visa, and I was flying back to New York via London. Flying back from Europe is always during the day, and I did not sleep, so I had a lot of time to think about Vera and our time together in the past few weeks. When I was going to the Kennedy Airport on the way to Yugoslavia, I was fearing the unknown: will my big plans be accomplished, and how would everything turn out? Now that everything turned out just the way I envisioned what would happen, the worry was still with me on the way back to the United States, mostly about Vera being left behind. One comforting thing was that she would be coming with my uncle and aunt, and they would wait there as long as it took until she got her entry visa.

As soon as I got back, I had to go to work. This time around, I did not mind going to work. In fact, I was looking forward to telling my story to friends and coworkers about my vacation and my venture into getting married. Going to and from work was still a big worry for me because the race riots continued throughout the hot summer of 1965 with no end in sight.

A few weeks after my return from Europe, I had to report to the army reserve for two weeks of training at Fort Drum, New York. At this time, I found myself in the army uniform again but under different circumstances, where the experience and my higher rank made my training much more pleasant. On one occasion, I was speaking with the commanding officer, and I mentioned that I just got married in Yugoslavia and that my wife was waiting for an entry visa to join me in the States. Without much thought, the officer advised me to write a letter while still in reserve to a senator from New York and explain my situation of hardship for being separated from my wife because of my duty in the army reserves. I was very thankful for his great advice, and I went after this immediately. With some help from the staff in the office on the army base, I addressed the letter to Robert F. Kennedy, a freshman senator from the State of New York, listing all my difficulties of being separated from my wife due to my active duty, while serving in the army reserve. I pleaded for his help to speed up the issuance of an entry visa for Vera so she could join me soon in New York City. I had high hopes for help from Senator Kennedy, but I did not expect results anytime soon. Due to the heavy training, my mind was so occupied that it did not leave me much time to think about anything else, which let the time pass by much faster. It was just two days before I received orders of discharge when I received a reply letter from Senator Kennedy, thanking me for the service to the country and stating that his staff would look into the review of Vera's application for an entry visa.

I just completed two weeks of training in the army reserve and returned home to New York City to resume my work in the Stimpson Company. Also, this was the time for my second school year to start. The heavy pressure was back on me again, where I was working all day and going to school at night, but that was what I wanted, as I knew that would not be forever.

My first day of school meant so much to me: to reunite with my classmates and, of course, my good Polish friend Edy. I had so much to tell Edy, as he also wanted to know everything about my trip to Yugoslavia and me getting married. His life also changed through the summer, a final divorce from his German wife, and he met Anna, the Polish girl. These conversations between us were going on all the time while we were progressing nicely in our class of mechanical drafting. It was nearing the end of September 1965 when Vera received a call from the American embassy in Belgrade with information that her visa was ready to be issued. Vera packed her things, and with an emotional goodbye to her family and friends in Petrovac, she went to Belgrade to pick up her visa and wait for my uncle and aunt to purchase airline tickets for all of them. The final day arrived, October 29, 1965, when Vera with my uncle and aunt were flying to New York. These were very exciting moments for me, and I remember that day very well. I got up very early that morning, cleaned the house and the car as much as I could, went to the store, and purchased nice flowers to take with me to the airport. When I got to the airport, I had to wait for the Pan Am flight to arrive at the international terminal, where I felt like the minutes looked like hours to wait. Finally, the passengers started coming out, and after a while, I spotted Vera with my uncle and aunt. Very hard to describe my feelings at that time, as one thing was for sure: my Vera had arrived, and we were finally together. Vera was very happy to see me, but I did not know how she was going to adjust to the new surroundings and the way of life in the US. After all, for the first time in her life, she went so far away from her home and her family and friends to share her life with me. This was not an easy task by any imagination. Finally, we got home from the airport, and Vera and I encroached on a new beginning of our life together in the United States of America.

At this time, my life got a little more complex. In addition to my day job at Stimpson Company and the evening school, there was very little time left to spend with my wife. Vera was staying home with my aunt and uncle, watching TV and learning English, more or less the same as I did when I arrived in the States. My aunt Maria did not always come across as an understanding and kind person, so Vera started getting uneasy feelings just when she needed more comfort during this difficult time of transition. I was faced with a very difficult decision to make: how to solve this problem but to make sure not to damage my relationship with my uncle and aunt. The decision was the right one. We rented a one-bedroom apartment ten minutes away from walking distance. We furnished our new apartment with inexpensive furniture, and we had everything we needed at that time. At the Stimpson Company, for over a year, I was looking for the opportunity to be transferred to the drafting department to pursue the coria of my passion. Finally, one day, I was called in by the supervisor to ask me questions about the progress in my school and stated that one draftsman was leaving the company and they would give me a chance to fill in this position if I performed to their satisfaction. When I heard these words, I nearly jumped out of my skin from joy and happiness, and that was how I got into the mechanical drafting position. I considered this position to be only a foot in the door for my dream of building coria in mechanical engineering. Now I was determined to perform more and better than ever to show gratitude for the opportunity they gave me. The knowledge gained already in the evening school aided me in my new drafting position, which made me excel at a much faster pace. When the customer requested a quotation for a certain part to be manufactured, they submitted a sample or a sketch of their part with information on quantity and the type of metal and finish required. This information would be submitted to our drafting department to make our own standard drawing with accurate tolerances and specifications required for the tool and die production. In addition to manufacturing metal fasteners, the Stimpson Company was also making attaching machines for inserting the fasteners to a product such as leather, canvas, clothing, footwear, etc. Any part submitted to production required a drawing with accurate dimensions. My experience in machine shop work and knowledge gained at the school helped me deal with the technical part of mechanical drawings.

It did not take very long for the drafting supervisor to recognize my good work and my striving for more knowledge. The mechanical engineer in the department was a

German immigrant, a brilliant mind but not very generous with sharing his knowledge with others. It took quite some time for him to warm up to me, but finally, he taught me many things that I could never learn from textbooks. On the home front, Vera became the family way, which brought more joy and happiness to our lives. Our apartment was located in a four-story building consisting of sixteen apartments. The owner of this building also owned the next-door building, also with six-teen apartments. The manager (superintendent) of these two buildings was planning to leave shortly after we moved in. Vera and I were interested in taking this job, and we contacted the owner to give us a chance. The owner was impressed with my handyman's capability and gave us the job. This side job was a big undertaking for me because it was in addition to my full-time job at Stimpson Company and still going to night school. We were determined to make it work, and we did. The compensation for this job was a free apartment and one hundred dollars per month. On the weekends and holidays, I did many extra repairs, and we maintained the buildings in better condition than any other manager before us. The winter months were the hardest as we had to maintain the heat in the buildings and clear the snow. I will never forget those winter days, coming back home from school around 11:00 p.m. and mopping four flight stairs in both buildings before going to bed. Even for a young man as I was at that time, this was something to remember for the rest of my life. The tenants in the building appreciated my hard work, and so did the owner of the buildings, who often rewarded us with extra money. Those days, we faced a lot of hard work and heavy responsibility, but we did not mind as we knew it would not be forever. Vera was nicely progressing in learning of English language, which made her better communicate with the tenants in the building when I was not around. She was still going through a period of adjustment in coping with everyday life in America. Our way of thinking was appreciably different in many ways from a typical young American born. Perhaps our growing up under difficult conditions and not having a normal childhood made us value more the opportunity of getting jobs and education for better advancement and a brighter future.

Vera and I entered a new chapter of our life with the arrival of our son Michael on September 20, 1966. Our priority immediately shifted, and from that day on, our lives changed forever. Not knowing much about parenting, we had to learn many things along the way. It was getting close to my graduation from Mechanics Institute. The school did not have its own hall, so the graduation ceremonies were held at United Engineering Center at United Nations Plaza, New York City. The program included an invocation by Rev. Horace W. Hughes, followed by an introductory address by Francis J. McCue and a main address by Timothy W. Costello, Deputy Mayor-City Administrator. Finally, diplomas were awarded by Louis H. Rouillion, the director of the Mechanics Institute. I was feeling very good about adding another achievement to my résumé. Many congratulations followed from family and friends, especially coworkers at Stimpson Company. Immediately after my graduation, I started exploring the possibilities to continue my education. At this time, I had more on my plate than I could handle, as I did not have any free time to go to school, but the drafting supervisor at work suggested that I investigate correspondence schools. I discovered that International Correspondence Schools from Scranton, Pennsylvania, was offering a course in machine design, including mechanics, mathematics, and drafting. Immediately, I signed into this program and used the GI Bill (post-military assistance) to pay for my tuition. Much of this study I was able to do at my job at Stimpson Company which helped me a lot. Since this was directly related to what I was doing at my work, the company was very supportive of me taking the course. By the spring of 1969, I had completed final exams and received a machine design diploma. This achievement resulted in an increase in my salary, which was very much needed at that time. I remember the department supervisor saying to me, "The baby needs new shoes." He was a very kind man and gave me many good advice not only related to my work but also general things in life.

Shortly after completing my machine design course, I was called into the main office by the company's president who was also the owner. I had no idea what this was about, but it made me very nervous. When I got to his office, he greeted me and asked me to sit down. At first, he congratulated me on my school achievement and wished me all the best in my work at Stimpson Company. The conversation shifted by describing to me the company's Florida division that was employing 350 employees and that there was a growing need for a drafting department to aid in manufacturing. Finally, he came out by offering me a transfer to Florida. I found myself in a very difficult position to give an answer, but I stated that I had never been to Florida and would have to discuss this matter with my wife and family. The president further asked if I would like to take my wife and son to Pompano Beach, Florida, for a week of vacation at a company expense to visit the plant and get acquainted with the surrounding area. It would be fine whenever I would like to do that, just to let him know. After careful consideration of the offer, Vera and I decided to make a trip to Florida, and only after that, evaluate what the move would mean to my career and, in general, the quality of life for my family in the new area. The president's son handled travel arrangements for me and my family.

When we got to the Kennedy Airport on the way to Ft. Lauderdale, Florida, Vera and I told each other that we liked Florida, even before we got there. That was our first indication of approval for our eventual move to Florida. Being that this was our first vacation together, we wanted it to be a very special one and to enjoy every minute off. Our son Michael was only three years old at the time. Upon our arrival at Ft. Lauderdale airport, we were greeted by the sales manager, whom I knew from New York, who was also transferred to Florida Plant recently. First, he took us to his house in Pompano Beach for a drink and to meet his wife, then he drove us to Stimpson, where I picked up the company car, and we were on our way to the hotel. The next day, in the morning, I went to visit the company while Vera and Michael stayed back to enjoy the swimming pool. At that time, the Stimpson Company was the largest manufacturing plant (250,000 sq. ft. facility) in Pompano Beach, with 350 employees. When I got to the plant, I had the pleasure of meeting Chairman of the Board, the twin brother of the company's president in New York. I knew him from his occasional trips to the New York plant and some other people who transferred recently from New York. I was taken on a factory tour by a plant manager, stopping at all departments for a brief description of the operation. Basically, all those departments were extensions from departments in New York. By then, I had nine years with the Stimpson Company, and I felt that I had good knowledge of the entire operation, and it made me feel at home.

The rest of the week, we did drive around to get familiar with the area, checking into real-estate, schools, beaches, and anything else that would help us make the final decision for a possible move to Pompano Beach. These were the days when was advertised from Miami in TV commercials with his famous saying, "Come on down." The state of Florida had a lot to offer with less expensive housing, no state income tax, and, in general cost of living was much better than in New York. Even so, these were the late sixties. We witnessed traces of discrimination on the beach, where African Americans had to use the north side of the fishing pier, but in time, equality was achieved. On our return to New York, we were faced with decision-making, whether to accept the company's offer on my relocation. This was not an easy task by any means, but after careful consideration of all the facts involved, we decided to make a move. When I reported back to the company's president, I thanked him for the opportunity he gave us to visit Florida and let him know that I would like very much to relocate, but, if possible, to delay some so I could get some of my personal things in order. He was very pleased to hear my decision and told me to take my time, just to let him know when I was ready. The only reason for the delay in our move was to save some money for a down payment on the house in Florida. When all these activities settled down, I became extremely anxious about my move to Florida and my future position in the company. There was a lot to think about, on the one hand, moving and settling down in the new surroundings, and on the other hand, my job itself. I knew that I was very good at the job I was doing, but forming a new drafting department meant also more responsibility and a bigger challenge ahead.

At that moment, I knew that more education was needed to be successful and not to disappoint my superiors. Immediately, I enrolled in an engineering class through the correspondence school from Scranton, Pennsylvania, where I obtained my machine design diploma. The company was paying for my tuition, so there was no financial burden from this undertaking. Having already so much experience at my work helped me accelerate my study, and I was passing the tests with flying colors.

The summer was over, and we were heading for another and perhaps last winter in the city of New York. Being that I was faced with so many activities, our social life was almost nonexistent, but occasionally, we managed to get together with Edy and Ana, our Polish friends. After graduation from the Mechanics Institute, Edy moved to

New City, New York, some thirty-five miles away from us. They had a lovely home on a small lake with beautiful surroundings that we enjoyed very much.

Branko and Vera (1969) at Restaurant Dubrovnik, in New York City.

On one occasion, at the wedding of a mutual friend, Vera and I met a new friend, Danilo Ivancevic, a countryman with so much in common, and we remained close friends to this day. A few years later, Danilo and his wife Marie moved to West Palm Beach, Florida.

Our last winter in New York City was brutal, with so much snow and bad weather that we felt as if we were being punished for the last time for going to the sunshine state of Florida. Finally, the spring was approaching, and I knew it was time to inform the company's president of me being ready to set a date for transfer to the Florida plant. The company arranged with movers for the beginning of May, which gave us ample time to tie loose ends and say final goodbye to friends and relatives. My uncle Steve was not very happy about us leaving New York, and he tried every possible way to change our decision, even offering us $3,000 to start some sort of business. Uncle Steve was my closest relative, and I was very appreciative of all he had done for me, but considering my job promotion, the future in Stimpson Company, and the quality of life for my family could not sway me from my decision to move. If I could summarize with one word my life in New York, it would be a challenging one, as I have lived through many firsts in my workplace, military, education, and social life, but the pride of my life was seeing my son Michael making first steps, saying first words, seeing first snow, and many other firsts that follow.

Finally, the day to leave was upon us. The movers picked up our furniture while we packed our car with the essentials that we needed for the trip, and we left New York City, heading south on our 1,200-mile journey. Those days, I-95 was not completed in many places, so by taking alternate routes, we enjoyed the scenery, but it slowed us down considerably. Also, Michael was only four years old, so we had to make frequent stops. We had a new car, a 1969 Ford LTD, which made our trip very comfortable. On the way down, we spent two nights in a motel, and on the third day, midmorning, we arrived at our destination, Stimpson Company, in Pompano Beach, Florida. I had to go to the company to pick up the apartment key that the company provided until we got situated. The Stimpson Company owned a duplex (two furnished apartments) for the use of relocation of their employees. The apartment was in a very nice community, with practically new furnishings, so we enjoyed it very much. I was told to take the rest of the week off for some rest from the trip before returning to work. The beach was less than a mile away, so it did not take us much time before our visit. Those days, there were not many tourists visiting Florida, so the beaches were rather empty, but certainly, it was the beginning of the large population growth for the years ahead. Just to put it in perspective, the state of Florida's population in 1970 was seven million, while in 2020, it reached twenty-two million. I lived through that fifty-year boom of population explosion and witnessed firsthand the rapid growth of Florida cities.

Finally, Monday had arrived for me to return to work and face the challenge of new duties. At first, I reported to the personnel department, as it was called those days, for orientation and briefing on some local rules and regulations of Stimpson Company. At that time, the Florida plant was mainly manufacturing buildings with rather small office buildings in front where all administrative activities were conducted, such as human resources, purchasing, payroll, sales, and private office for the plant manager and chairman of the board (owner). In the factory building, there was a temporary office set up for advertising and marketing, and then an additional office had to be added to house the drafting department. The company was planning to build a new office building in front of the factory for all administrative and technical personnel, including private offices.

I was fine with this arrangement, as I knew it would not be for a very long time. From the very first day, I worked with the purchasing manager to furnish this new department with all the equipment needed, starting with desks, chairs, drafting boards, tables, a blueprint machine, and all the tools and supplies required to produce and process drawings. Up to this point, all drawings and technical information for the manufacturing was furnished by the New York plant through fax or truck delivery. All raw materials for the production in the Florida plant and returning finished goods to New York were transported by Stimpson trucks once or twice a week, so the driver would also carry all the correspondence between the plants.

While I was setting up my department, I had a chance to meet with some department heads and other personnel whom I knew from the New York Plant who relocated to Florida before me. As I was eager to start working, it did not take me long to show my skills and really engage in technical assistance in the manufacturing of our metal stamping goods. In addition to making drawings with all the specifications of a finished product, there was a need for drawings for the tool and die department to make tooling to produce finished goods. Anyone with knowledge of tool and die operation in the metal stamping industry knows how precise precision and accuracy are important. Day-to-day operations were becoming routine, and I enjoyed helping the foremen and supervisors resolve technical issues. After several weeks of living in the company's furnished apartment, we decided to rent from Ft. Lauderdale Beach while we were still exploring the area where to buy a new home.

Summertime in Florida was not popular for tourists, so the furnished apartments along the beach area were very reasonable for us to take advantage of the situation. Living by the beach was paradise for us. Michael and Vera loved it too.

Since the company was in Pompano Beach, our main focus on buying a home was in that area, with a good school and near the ocean. While driving through Pompano Beach one weekend, we came upon a near-completion duplex with a sign for sale. The builder had just finished one apartment and rented it out to a nice family while putting the finishing touches on the other apartment. The building was Mediterranean style, with three bedrooms and two baths for each apartment, which was exactly what we were looking for. The price was more than we could afford at the time, but with the help of my uncle from New York, we managed to put together enough money for a down payment, and the rest financed with a bank mortgage. It was more expensive than a single-family home, but considering living in one apartment and the rental income from the other apartment was enough to cover the mortgage payment. We felt that our decision was a wise investment. Since the move, our furniture has been in storage, waiting for the purchase of a new home, and upon the closing, we had it delivered. The house was close to Pompano Fashion Square, which was developed in 1970 as the first regional shopping hub in Broward County. The kindergarten for Michael was only a block away, and the beach was less than a mile away. The Stimpson Company was only three miles from our home, a far cry from our situation in New York, where I had to spend hours going to and from work. By purchasing a duplex, we instantly became landlords, something that we were not planning for, but the additional income was a great help at a time when we needed it the most.

At work, I was progressing nicely and getting along with everyone. Mostly, I enjoyed helping shop personnel with many technical issues in the various projects they were involved with. One of the departments that I was helping a lot with was machine repair, which was repairing and maintaining all the production and nonproduction equipment in the plant. One of the best machinists in the department was Fernando Luciani, whom I called Freddy, a recent Italian immigrant from Switzerland. As we got to know each other much better, we became very good friends. Freddy's wife, Irma, a German immigrant, worked in the tool and die department for the same company. At that time, they were the only close friends that we had in Florida, and we became frequent visitors to each other's homes. This was a similar situation that I had in New York when I met a Polish friend through the school, and then in Florida, we met German and Italian, who remained our friends to this very day.

Our departure from New York did not sit well with my Uncle Steve, as he missed us very much. He decided to visit us to see how we were doing and what Florida looked like. He was very happy to see us, and to our big surprise, he liked the living conditions in Florida and stated that he would not mind moving from New York.

After a couple of years of living in the duplex, we were able to save some money with the intention of building a single-family home. Some ten miles west of Pompano Beach, the new community of Coral Springs was being developed by Westinghouse. We went to see their model homes, and one that we liked the most was a four-bedroom Mediterranean style. Once again, we did not have enough money to put down for the construction of this beautiful home. We used our ingenuity and came up with a great idea to refinance the mortgage on our duplex and use that equity toward the new home. Signing the contract with the builder for the construction of a new home was the biggest undertaking so far in our lives. Since Michael was only six years old, Vera could not have a full-time job, so she went to work part-time in the evenings at the Jordan Marsh retail store, and I would be with Michael at home. Working even part-time was good for Vera, not only for financial help but also to get out of the house. About this time, our friends Freddy and Irma decided to sell their home and permanently move to live in Bergamo, North Italy. Since we became good friends, their decision to leave the United States was very disappointing to us, but we pledged to each other that we would be in contact and visit in the future.

Shortly after that, our friends from New York, Edy and Ana, visited us in Pompano Beach and fell in love with Florida. Upon their return to New York, they decided to sell their home in New City, New York, and move to Coral Springs, Florida, close to where we were planning to build our new home. In the early seventies, the Stimpson Company's main facility and headquarters, located in

Brooklyn, New York, was relocating its entire plant to the town of Bayport in Long Island, New York. Many employees who did not wish to move to Bayport were given the opportunity to relocate to the Florida plant in Pompano Beach. Once the transfer of employees and equipment was completed, the company sold the old buildings that they had owned since 1852. All those employees who transferred to Florida I personally knew, and many of them were my good friends, so I was able to offer them guidance for good locations of housing and good schools. The manufacturing was steadily increasing, and the company had to keep up with the purchase of new equipment to stay ahead of the competition in the metal stamping industry.

In 1970, during the Nixon Administration, the US Congress enacted the Occupational Safety and Health Administration (OSHA) for the protection of workers in the workplace. From the first day of this new law, our company started implementing the changes, and I was involved in all technical aspects of the change. I remember very well one instance where the output of air pressure in all air guns had to be drastically reduced. Hundreds of these air guns were used for blowing the metal chips in the machining process of tooling and general cleaning through the plant. Instead of purchasing all new guns to meet OSHA specifications, I studied the construction of the gun and came up with a redesign of one part to restrict the air supply, which gave me the required safety output and saved the company from purchasing all new parts. The new law covered all aspects of manufacturing, and we had to reduce excessive noise levels in the power press departments by installing certain barriers between the presses to bring the sound to a required level. Being the only technical person in the plant gave me the opportunity to work on many other projects outside my duties and the drafting department. Sometimes, I would study different manufacturing operations to see if I could come up with a better approach to a safer and faster way of production. One of my major projects at the time was the redesign of a brake system on a roll feed attachment for the stamping press. Roll feed attachment is the mechanism for feeding a metal strip into the progressive die of a stamping press. One component of this attachment is the brake system, traditionally two bands around the disc spring loaded. During off hours, the press lubricating fluids and oil would settle in the brake bands and cause sticking problems. Each morning, the mechanics had to clean up the brake bands prior to starting up, which was time-consuming and loss of production. I came up with a totally different approach by introducing the disc brake, operated by the air pressure, so when the press was turned off, it caused the brake to disengage and stay free of lubricants and oil. The management approved this design, and we retrofitted hundreds of roll feeds with the new disc brake system.

As I was getting more engaged in my work and spending all my free time with my son Michael while Vera was working in the evenings, my schoolwork slowed somewhat. Despite all this activity, I managed to take all the tests and successfully completed and received in April of 1973 the certificate of the mechanical engineering division one.

Immediately, I enrolled in division two and the final part of Mechanical Engineering.

The management of Stimpson Company was very pleased with my achievement and rewarded me with a pay raise.

Those days, in the early seventies, the slide rule was still being used to calculate multiplication and division and for functions such as exponents, roots, logarithms, and trigonometry. During the space program in the sixties, many good new technologies came out to benefit mankind, such as the birth of a calculator and computer. I was the first person in the company to receive the Texas Instruments calculator and, later in the eighties, the very first Apple Macintosh 512K computer. The use of these new instruments made my life much easier to perform many different tasks that I was working on. Of course, the slide rule became obsolete. One of the most essential tools to produce drawings was a table with a drafting machine attached to it. The drafting machine consisted of two scales attached to a protractor head mechanism ninety degrees apart for sliding on a table in the horizontal or vertical direction. In the late eighties, the drafting machine was replaced too with a computer-aided design by new AutoCAD Software. I was very fortunate that the company saw the benefits of these new technologies and made it possible for me to equip the drafting department with the latest. It meant so much to me, not only for being the first in the company to receive this equipment but also for living through the times of the computer technology explosion.

The construction of our new house was finished, and we moved in December of 1974 just for Christmas. Just after Christmas school break, Michael started the second part of second grade at Westchester Elementary School in Coral Springs. This was one of the best elementary schools in Broward County. Michael was an exceptionally good student, and he was placed in a gifted program so he could excel in his studies at a much faster pace.

Our Polish friends, Edy and Ana, had a house not far from us, and we were getting together every Friday evening. We were very good friends, so it felt like we were family. After all, we were the godparents of their daughter Christina. Edy was also a mechanical engineer, so we had so much in common. Also, Vera and Ana were good friends, not to mention that our Michael was getting along very well with Henry and Christina, their children. Ana was very creative in mixing drinks. Whenever we got together, she would make a different kind of drink. I will never forget one occasion when Ana combined raw egg and scotch whiskey in a blender to make a super great drink. We were young, and anything could go, but those were the memories that one never forgot. For all the major holidays, we went together somewhere. Our most popular destination was Sanibel Island on the West Coast of Florida, on a great beach with lots of privacy, and the kids loved it.

The city of Coral Springs was very popular for sports activities where children of all ages could join programs in all sports. In the past, playing soccer was not very popular in the United States, but it all changed when the Brazilian soccer legend Pele joined the New York Team Cosmos of the

North American Soccer League in 1975. Pele even visited South Florida, and the interest among youngsters exploded with the love for the game. Being that I grew up with soccer, which was the number one sport in Europe, made me volunteer to be a soccer coach for one of the teams where my son Michael was playing. Perhaps I enjoyed it just as much as kids did playing, and it lasted for several seasons. Michael also played football, where all teams were ranked by age group, and he continued playing sports throughout his middle school years. After Michael graduated from middle school with high honors, we wanted to make sure that he continued in high school with the best possible rating. His close friends were planning to attend St. Thomas Aquinas, the private parochial school that was twenty-five miles away and did have the school bus available for our area. The school tuition with the bus service was very high for our income bracket, but we were determined that Michael got the best possible education and to better prepare him for college. With those added expenses, it was clear to me that I had to look for a second job in order to provide enough income to cover Michael's education.

Back in the spring of 1975, I received a degree in mechanical engineering that gave me enough education to qualify me to receive the teacher's certificate in the field of drafting and blueprint reading. With all my supporting documents, I applied for a teaching certificate through the state of Florida Department of Education, and in a very short time, I got a teaching position in the Coral Springs High School Adult Program in the evening classes. In the seventies and eighties, there was a great expansion in

Florida's population, and many new communities were springing up all over South Florida. There was a shortage of skilled labor, and the adult program for all trades was designed to alleviate this problem. I was teaching the class mechanical drafting and architectural blueprint reading and estimating twice a week for each subject. This was not an easy job for me by any means, having a full daytime job and part-time in the evening, but it was a great financial help. I was amazed to find out that some of my students were building contractors without sufficient knowledge of blueprint reading. That, of course, affected the estimates of their jobs. I must say that this kind of work gave me personal satisfaction in helping others to achieve their goal by becoming more proficient in the job they do.

In the seventies, there was encouragement by the US government to move from the US measuring system and convert it into a global metric system. The US Congress passed the Metric Conversion Act of 1975, which triggered many meetings throughout the United States. There was a pro and against the conversion among many industries and unions, mainly who was going to bear the cost of retooling America. Since I grew up with the metric system in Europe, I applied for membership in the Metric Association of America to be fully informed on the progress of the conversion. One year, the Carpenter Union of Ohio was holding their meeting in Fort Lauderdale, Florida, and I was contacted by the board of education with an offer to be the speaker to the Carpenter Union members to lecture on the benefits of the metric system. With great reluctance, I accepted the offer, which gave me some worry because I never spoke to a large group like that. I prepared myself with all the facts and benefits of the standards with the metric system, and the meeting went very well. Unfortunately, due to many reasons, the United States was not ready to go metric, and the whole initiative was abolished in 1982 by President Ronald Reagan.

In the late seventies, the Stimpson Company was heavily investing in automation by purchasing new equipment and redesigning old production methods. With my engineering capacity, I played a very important part in the purchase of new equipment and the redesign of old production lines throughout the facility.

In 1982, the company's president, who was located in the main office in New York, came down to Florida for a meeting, mainly regarding the advertising department whose manager was retiring. I was called to the meeting where the president praised my work and my involvement in the automation of the production process. It was followed by offering me to take over the advertising department, in addition to overseeing the drafting department. I must say, this was a great surprise to me, and I was totally unprepared for how to react to this unexpected offer. I told the president that I had not done this kind of work in the past and that I was not sure if I would be able to deliver the results that they expected. The president was quick to say, you know the product more than anyone else, and after a while, if you do not want this, you still have the drafting department. He went on further to assure me of his support and that I would be able to attend any seminar nationwide related to advertising. I gratefully thanked him for giving me the opportunity for this additional responsibility and that I would do my best to promote the image and profit of the company in the years to come. This was a day to remember, and I could not wait to come home to tell my wife, Vera, what had happened to me. Someone would think I was lucky, but my theory is that there is no such thing as being lucky; instead, everyone is making their own luck by doing or not doing the right thing. From that day forward, I knew that I was embarking on something bigger than I had ever done before in my life. Much was at stake, but being the positive person that I am, there was no doubt in my mind that I would not be able to accomplish what I was about to start.

The outgoing advertising manager stayed on for a while, giving me the opportunity to get acquainted with the staff and the entire operation of the department. The advertising department produced the ads to be placed in many technical publications, product catalogs of the entire product line to be printed, the company's stationery, and all other printing matters. Also, the department maintained a list of some forty thousand customers and prospects for the periodic mailings with promotional product literature. I was no stranger to the workers in the department as I knew many of them back in New York before they transferred to Florida. It was very important to me that each employee in the department was well placed in the position that they knew most about and to make sure that I was surrounded by the best possible staff to make my life easier.

I found myself wearing two hats, and, if I may say, much different because advertising and drafting are entirely different approaches to achieving the results. Engineering results are always based on factual calculation, while advertising and marketing can even deviate some time from facts and still achieve good results through spirited and guided emotions. In those days, there was no computer-aided ad production, so to produce an ad for publications, one had to have basic skills in layout and pasteup in addition to a good knowledge of photography. I attended my first ten-day seminar in Atlanta, Georgia, for building skills in layout and pasteup with some photography. A few months later, I attended another seminar in Philadelphia, Pennsylvania, on marketing objectives. These seminars gave me much-needed theoretical and practical basic knowledge of advertising and marketing skills, but most of all, they gave me the opportunity to meet with my peers to exchange ideas and see how others approach these issues.

Stimpson Company's annual budget was set to approximately half a million dollars for placing various ads of the product line in technical publications to reach engineers and shop supervisors. There were two major publishing houses, Penton Publishing out of Cleveland, Ohio, and Cahners Publishing out of Boston, Massachusetts. Both Penton and Cahners were publishing several magazines for various trades, and they were competitors to each other, so it was very important for me to study which magazine produced more prospects and, according to that information, placed the number of ads and frequency to run in each publication. My job was to prepare the annual advertising proposal for the number of ads to run in each publication with the amount of money needed to accomplish good results and present it to the president of the company for his approval. Usually, in the fall of every year, I would be visited by publisher's representatives to work on the annual advertising contracts.

In February of each year, the city of Chicago held National Manufacturing Week with exhibitions and seminars (as we called it, the trade show) in the east and the west halls of McCormick Place. Stimpson Company was also exhibiting its products. Through the drafting department, I was performing all the engineering functions for the company, and the management gave me the opportunity to attend this trade show each year for the following twenty-five years until my retirement in July 2006. My main reason for going to the trade show was to look for any new ideas that could be applied to our company and to increase production while simplifying the process. Fortunately for me, this was one of the best sources of new ideas, with cutting-edge new technologies exhibited each year. The Stimpson Company had an exhibition booth at the trade show where the salesmen from different parts of the country would be attendees. I had the opportunity to meet with them and discuss our marketing strategy. Through our advertising program, we were generating prospects that were channeled to the salesmen for further follow-up. With our salesmen, I was very comfortable as I knew most of them from our New York office.

At our home front, Michael was nearing high school graduation, and Vera decided to seek employment at Stimpson Company. I spoke with the plant manager regarding this matter, and Vera was immediately hired to work as a shipping clerk. This was very advantageous for us, as we were able to travel together to and from work.

Finally, Michael graduated from high school and immediately started looking into colleges where he would like to proceed with his ambition to study nuclear engineering. He found out that Florida University at Gainesville, Florida, had a good nuclear engineering program, and he applied and was accepted. This was all a new challenge for Michael, but in a way for me and Vera, too, as the big financial burden was upon us, but we wanted more than anything else to make sure that he finished college to set him on a path to a much better future. We were very proud of Michael and his accomplishments so far, and that was just the beginning of what was coming in the years ahead.

At the beginning of the eighties, we discovered the Serbian Orthodox Church in Miami, about thirty miles away from our home in Coral Springs. The church was established in 1979, mostly by American-born Serbs, to serve the religious needs of Orthodox people who immigrated from different parts of Yugoslavia. At the time, a small group of parishioners purchased a private home where the religious service could take place every Sunday. As time went by, more Serbian families were moving to South Florida, and the church capacities had to be increased. Fortunately, the parishioners with different trades donated time and materials to add space to this house to meet the needs of the community. From the beginning, we did not go to church very often because of the distance from home and other activities that I was engaged in at the time. Vera and I both grew up in Communist Yugoslavia, where the religion was not practiced very much, so going to church service was not one of our priorities. During those years, my uncle Steve and aunt Maria lived in Hollywood, Florida, much closer to the church, so they attended Sunday services every week. Up to this time, we did not have friends from the old country, but now through the church activities, we started meeting some countrymen, even from our home state of Montenegro. Now through the church, our social time had increased, so I really do not know how we managed any of this. Of course, our friends Edy and Freddy, with their families, remained at the top of the list.

For the years ahead, I will give some more details about our future involvement with the church. With my political views, I was not always on the same page with my friends and coworkers, but I learned a long time ago to respect others views because we live in a country where freedom of expression is guaranteed. Ever since I came to the United States, I felt blessed to live in a country where democracy and freedom were embedded in Western values of everyday life. Those values were built on a premise of hard work and, most of all, the opportunity to become whatever your heart desires. Fortunately for me and my positive thinking, with my ups and downs in life, I continued to march forward through my life to get as much accomplished as possible. Stimpson Company gave me that chance to advance myself and create a better life for me and my family.

The company was a member of the Pompano Beach Chamber of Commerce, and my position as advertising manager required me to participate in local activities. During those years, the chamber was very active in promoting tourism in the area and helping the city with many incentives to bring in new companies and increase all kinds of business. Through the members' donations, the chamber sponsored monthly breakfast meetings to bring the business community together and present their needs to the city politicians. I always attended those meetings, which gave me the opportunity to meet many company representatives as well as city officials. These activities continued for years, and I became very much involved in the works of the chamber. So in 2003, I was nominated to serve on the board of directors. I remained in this position until my retirement in 2006. Personally, it made me very proud to serve on the chamber's board of directors and, at the same time, represent my company very well in the community.

Now that Michael, our son, was away from home and attending college in Gainesville, Florida, we got an idea to sell our home in Coral Springs and move closer to the ocean. In 1988, we did just that: we sold our home and temporarily moved into our rental property in Pompano Beach while we were looking for suitable permanent residence. Now we found ourselves again in the duplex, the property we purchased when we first arrived in Florida. Being that we were renting this property, the building needed repairs, and while there, we made renovations.

The neighboring city of Lighthouse Point was a very well-established and prestigious community that got our attention, and about a year later, in 1989, we purchased another house. This house also needed lots of work. We renovated and added a swimming pool. Now we were much closer to the beach and our work. Shortly after we moved into the house, Michael was graduating from college. That year, Vera's sister Ljubica from Budva, Montenegro, was visiting us, and we all together went to Gainesville to attend Michael's graduation. We were proudly witnessing Michael's achievements and getting a degree in nuclear engineering. This was the end of the winter semester, one of the coldest years on record. Driving from Gainesville that night on the way home, it was snowing, and the road conditions were getting worse. I remembered the highway patrol was closing I-95 after me, making our car the last one on the road halfway home.

In the last year of Michael's college, he was selected among fifteen other students from all over the United States for internship study in Washington, DC, and at the end of two months, to prepare the final report. Michael chose to do the study of nuclear standardization in the United States. He did such an outstanding study and compiled a final report that was circulated among many government agencies. It got attention from the Nuclear Regulatory Commission in Washington, DC, and after graduation, Michael was offered, and he accepted the position of nuclear engineer in the agency. One could only imagine how proud Vera and I were of Michael's achievements.

This meant that Michael was to move away from us and start his own destiny. Ever since childhood, Michael was very independent and knew what he wanted and how to get it, which gave us the comfort of knowing that he would be all right. This young man was ready to go, moved to Washington, DC, started employment with the agency of the Nuclear Regulatory Commission, and after thirty

THE JOURNEY OF MY LIFE

years, he was still there with many great accomplishments of his own. Vera and I continued living in South Florida.

Shortly after Michael's graduation, we learned that my uncle Spiro's health was deteriorating, and we decided to visit him in Montenegro, still Yugoslavia at that time. During this time, early nineties, Yugoslavia was engulfed in a full-blown war, mainly Serbs against Croatia and Muslims in Kosovo and Bosnia, spearheaded by Slobodan Milosevic and his supporters. To stop the madness, "NATO" (North Atlantic Alliance) had to intervene, and we all know how it ended. My heart goes out to all victims, regardless of race or nationality, as it was senseless and could have been avoided if there had been the right leadership. Fortunately for the Republic of Montenegro, with the leadership of Milo Djukanovic, the citizens were spared of this aggression and the very stiff sanctions that followed. There were no flights leaving or going to Belgrade, so we had to book a flight to Budapest, Hungary, and go by land transportation to Belgrade and then fly on to Montenegro. Arriving at the Hungarian-Yugoslav border, we were met with a very hostile border agent giving us a hard time for not having a visa to enter Yugoslavia. Even so we were born there and had ID cards, but we traveled on US passports. Since we were traveling by bus, all other passengers had to wait until we got permission to enter the country. It took more than an hour until I realized that the border agent was looking for some money, so I pulled a twenty-dollar bill and the agent immediately stamped our passports, and our bus was on the way to Belgrade. This was a very tiring seven-hour bus ride, so on arrival in Belgrade, we booked a one-night hotel so we could use it for a few hours to freshen up before our flight to Montenegro.

When we got there, Uncle and Aunt were very happy to see us. Uncle Spiro was in bad shape, and it was just a matter of time before leaving us to a better place. Vera and I were very happy that we were able to make this trip to see him for the last time. We could only stay for a few weeks as we had to return to our jobs. Almost a month after our return home, Uncle Spiro passed away in his eighty-seventh year, and a month after, my aunt Maria also passed away in her eighty-fourth year. We were not able to go back to Montenegro for the funeral, so my cousin Gojko, who lived in Petrovac, took care of funeral arrangements as well as all other details after their passing. In addition to our house in the village (my birthplace), Uncle left us a studio apartment where they lived in Petrovac, which we used several years for our Montenegro vacation trips.

Back at home in Florida, we got much more involved with our church, so in 1995, I was elected the president of the St. Simeon Parish in Miami. The Serbian community was steadily growing, and the heavy pressure was on me and the board members to start planning expansion to meet the church's needs in the years to come. As in any organization, internal politics were very much present, with people who thought they knew it all, with people who wanted to involve friends for self-benefit, and there were those people who mattered very much who came from different parts of Yugoslavia. Perhaps for me, too, being born in Montenegro, I was not always accepted by some born in proper Serbia. One could hear jokes that always sound nice but carry a heavy sting to it, for Montenegrins being lazy, Bosnians stupid, and so on. This did not bother me until later years because I was always proud of the address I came from. People from different regions of Yugoslavia have similarities but are not the same, as they are distinguished by their dialect, national costumes, names, and, in some cases, even looks. I personally resent when someone says we are all the same. When you hear those words "we are the same," you can be sure they are using it for their own personal gain. With military experience, management skills, and serving on the board of directors for the Pompano Beach Chamber of Commerce gave me the advantage. That is the knowledge to navigate through the internal church politics and accomplish what I was set to do. Those were very difficult times to raise money for the much-needed expansion of the church facility. The many parishioners were helping relatives and friends in Serbia as the country was under heavy international sanctions due to the wars created by Slobodan Milosevic. In spite of all the difficulties in raising funds, during my three-year presidency, we managed to purchase and pay for a large piece of land adjacent to the church property, which gave us possibilities for expansion. In addition to the normal church activities, the board organized many social events such as lunches every Sunday, church festivities, as well as musical events by bringing musicians from Chicago and other cities with large Serbian populations. The very first thing on the agenda was to plan and build a large church hall to use for temporary church and social activities until we realized the necessary funds to build the church next to the hall. I had some connections, and we hired the architect to plan and make drawings to submit to the building department of Miami-Dade County for permits to start with the construction. While I was heavily involved in the day-to-day running of the church, Vera worked very hard in organizing the kitchen to prepare the food for never-ending social activities. I must say that we were getting tired of all this, as this was in addition to our home and managing rental properties that we had.

After three years, another president took over the church parish and continued where I had left off, but I remained as a church board member until my retirement. So Vera and I proudly gave thirty years of our service to the St. Simeon church community in Miami.

In 1996, our son Michael was engaged to Rani Lee, and they planned to have a civil wedding with her parents in Virginia Beach and a church wedding in my birthplace in Montenegro. Vera and I were very happy with their decision and immediately started planning our trip. Those days, most international flights to Montenegro were going through Belgrade, Serbia, which made it more complicated by spending more travel time and overnighting in Belgrade. We have friends and relatives in Belgrade, so it gave us a chance to spend some time with them. Michael and Rani were working for the Nuclear Regulatory Commission in Rockville, Maryland, but at that time, they had a five-year assignment as residents in a nuclear plant near Charlotte, North Carolina. We had to fly separately, them from Charlotte and Vera and I from Miami to Belgrade and the second day, on to Tivat, Montenegro. Michael and Rani had only two weeks of vacation, so we had to move very fast with wedding arrangements.

The local priest found out that Rani was of Episcopal Faith, and he informed us that the marriage could only take place if Rani converted to Eastern Orthodoxy, to which Rani agreed. She was baptized a few days before the wedding. The wedding ceremony was officiated in the Monastery of Rezevici near Petrovac, Montenegro, in the presence of the family and many local friends. This wedding generated even more interest among the locals, as it was the very first church ceremony performed at the Monastery of Rezevici since (1939) just before the Second World War due to the Communist system. The reception for fifty guests was held in Hotel Palas. Michael and Rani wanted this to be a very small affair with family present only. This was impossible for us, and it took some convincing to do because Vera and I were born and raised in this town, so practically, the whole town was our friends that we could not ignore on such an important day of our only son's wedding. The smallest invitation list that we could put together was fifty guests. After the wedding, Michael and Rani did some travel through Montenegro and finally, as a married couple returned to Charlotte, North Carolina. Vera and I remained in Montenegro for a few weeks more to spend some time with family and friends before our return home to Florida. This was one unimaginable accomplishment for our son's wedding in a short time and so far away from home. Coming back home meant going back to work and continuing volunteer work at church as well as the local community.

Among the Serbian population of South Florida, there were some families from Montenegro, naturally in much smaller numbers, that tended to be always together on all church occasions. Back home, Yugoslavia fell apart, so all Republics claimed independence except Serbia and Montenegro, which lingered together until 2006. I started getting feelings of forming some sort of Montenegro group, a club, or something like that. I talked to several friends, and they felt the same way, so we got invited to the house of our mutual friend Danilo Ivancevic in West Palm Beach to further discuss this matter. That day, we all had the same feelings and agreed to schedule an organizational meeting and get things started.

So the small group of nine Montenegrins met on March 23, 1997, to form the very first Montenegrin Cultural Society Njegos in the state of Florida. The meeting took place in the restaurant of Rusty Pelican, Key Biscayne, Florida, with the help of its manager and our countryman Peter Knezevic. I wanted to be the secretary of the newly formed organization, and I maintained that position through the years. It gave me the opportunity to run the administration of the society. Later that year, we incorporated the society in the state of Florida as a nonprofit organization and designed the webpage and Facebook so we could list all our activities for everyone to see and follow. The purpose of the society was to promote the culture and customs as well as fellowships of the Montenegrin people living in South Florida. This was a huge undertaking for us that required sacrifice of a lot of time and financial support to get the organization started. This undertaking was not well received among some people in the Serbian community, and labeling us as separatists was further from the truth, and we proved it through the years. The brunt of criticism was directed toward me as they saw me as a person behind the formation of the Montenegrin Society. Our activities consisted of monthly gatherings such as dinners, day trips, cruises, musical events, etc. The most popular activity was the annual picnic that we scheduled for February of each year. One of the biggest achievements was that the attendees to our activities were the people from all the republics from ex-Yugoslavia, which proved us more as a group to unite people rather than separate them. I am very proud of my involvement in this society throughout the years until my leaving the state of Florida in November of 2020.

The years were marching on, and I was getting close to my retirement. Vera is four years younger than me, so she could retire at the age of sixty-two years old but with reduced benefits. We calculated income from all our assets and determined that we could live comfortably in our retirement, even with Vera's reduced pension. The decision was made that we both retire at the same time, and the date was set for July 1, 2006, ending my forty-six years of employment with the Stimpson Company and Vera's twenty-eight years. This decision was not an easy one, but looking back on my achievements through the years of my employment, I proudly accepted this decision and moved in stride forward to my golden years. At the time of my retirement, I was one of the longest-serving employees in the company, with great appreciation from the management. My deep gratitude goes to the owners of Stimpson Company for putting their trust in me to manage the drafting and advertising departments.

Now Vera and I found ourselves in retirement, which opened a new chapter of our life. No question about it. There were some adjustments to be made to our daily routine activities, from getting up in the morning to going to bed at night. To celebrate our retirement, we planned a trip to Montenegro to visit our families and get much-deserved rest and relaxation. In Montenegro, we had a house in the village where I was born and a studio apartment in nearby Petrovac, where we stayed during our visits there. This was the year when Montenegro, by referendum, separated from Serbia and once again became an independent country as it was prior to joining the Kingdom of Serbs, Croats, and Slovenes in 1918 and then renamed Yugoslavia in 1929. For better or worse, by now, all ex-Yugoslavia republics have declared independence. I loved my Montenegro then and always will, making me very proud of the address I came from.

Our first vacation in retirement was truly enjoyable, and we pledged to do this every year. During our working years, we traveled to many interesting destinations within the North American Continent and Europe. In the United States, covering from entertaining Las Vegas to nature's wonders of Yosemite National Park, the Blue Ridge Mountains, the spectacle of Niagara Falls, and in between many other well-known places. In this hemisphere, outside the United States, we also made unforgettable trips to Canada, Mexico, Costa Rica, and Jamaica. In addition to land vacations throughout the years, we sailed on many cruise ships and visited all popular Caribbean destinations, including the Panama Canal. One time, we joined a group of twenty-six members from Chicago's Serbian Academic Cub and sailed to St. Thomas. Another time, we joined a larger group of 160 Serbs from the area of Cleveland, Ohio, and Toronto, Canada, sailing through the Eastern Caribbean. In this group were also our dear friends Mirko and Mara Soljaga from Cleveland. This group also brought along a full Serbian orchestra that provided late-night entertainment. One can only imagine what kind of atmosphere that was with 160 Serbs on board and its full orchestra playing popular songs and dances. The cruise to the Panama Canal was also one unforgettable experience. Previously, only vessels with a maximum width of 106 feet could enter the locks of the Panama Canal. Princess Cruises was the first cruise line to take guests through the Panama Canal in 1967. On October 26, 2017, marking its fiftieth anniversary, Caribbean Princess, with a width of 118 feet and 3,200 guests, was the first post-Panamax cruise ship to sail through the newly opened Agua Clara locks on the Atlantic side of the canal. Vera and I were among those guests on this inaugural sail.

In this hemisphere, one of the most memorable sails for us was in May of 2001, on the cruise to Alaska. Alaskan cruises operate only between the middle of May and the end of August due to the extreme weather conditions. We chose to go in May together with our friends Rade and Zora Vukadinovic, flying to Vancouver, Canada, and boarding on a Holland America cruise ship Statendam and sailing for seven days to the city port of Seward, then taking the land tour for five more days through Anchorage, Denali National Park and onto the city of Fairbanks before flying back home. On the first leg of our trip, we flew from Miami to Vancouver the day before boarding the ship. In Vancouver, we were greeted by my cousin Gojko's son Simo and his wife Olja, who permanently reside there. It was great to see them and spend some time together.

The next morning, we visited Stanley Park, with its beautiful gardens, overseeing the city of Vancouver. We got back to the hotel for lunch and boarded the ship in the afternoon hours. The Holland America cruise ships were known for their excellent service and for sure did not disappoint us. The ship was mostly sailing during the night and visiting interesting ports during the day. The city of Ketchikan was the first port on the southeastern coast of Alaska for the ship to dock. The meaning of Ketchikan is Salmon Creek, the original location of an Indian fishing camp. Taking a tour of the city, we came across local manufacturing of Totem poles and learned of its meaning. The Totem poles are monumental carvings on a large cedar wood post that tell the story of the family, clan, or village who own them. They are found in western Canada and the northwestern United States. The Totem Heritage Center, located in Ketchikan, was founded in 1976. It is open to the public where one can learn all about history and the making of Totem poles. Walking the streets of Ketchikan gave us the first taste of Alaska and subzero temperatures. We continued sailing on to another coastal city of Sitka, which has a ten-thousand-year-old history that began when

Tlingit people settled in Southeast Alaska. Once the capital of Russian America in 1808, Sitka was the site of the Alaska Purchase on March 30, 1867. That's when the United States bought Alaska from the Russians for $7.2 million. For us, one of the most interesting sites was St. Michael's Cathedral, also known as the Cathedral of St. Michael the Archangel. It is a cathedral of the Orthodox Church in America Diocese of Alaska. The earliest Orthodox cathedral in the New World was built in the nineteenth century when Alaska was under the control of Russia. We went on a tour of the cathedral and bought some souvenirs. Not far from the church, we also attended a show of a local folklore group performing Russian dances. In this city, there are no Russian residents anymore, but the locals are still preserving the culture of the people who once lived there. It was very nice to see, and we enjoyed the performance very much.

We went back to the ship and on the way to Juneau, the capital of Alaska, located in the Gastineau Channel, and the Alaskan panhandle with a population of thirty thousand people. Juneau is best known for Mendenhall Glacier and the Juneau Gold Rush of 1880. Unlike any other city in the United States, there are no roads connecting it to the rest of Alaska or North America. It is truly a protected destination reachable only by air or sea. Before we docked in Juneau, together with our friends, we booked an offshore helicopter tour, covering sixty-five miles of Alaska's wilderness and massive icefields, including landing on the glacier. This was an unforgettable experience and had to be the highlight of this journey. In addition to offshore tours, the ship's captain stopped the ship near a large glacier for the passenger's photo and watched the glacier "calve." In this process, large chunks of ice break off from the glacier and fall into the water. The smaller floating pieces of ice are called "bergy bits" that the ship is navigating through while sailing these icy waters. The ship continued to sail toward our final sea destination of Seward. Two days later, we docked in Seward, completing our seven days of sea adventure. At the dock, we were greeted by the ship tour guides to guide us to a prospective bus for a two and a half hour's ride north to the city of Anchorage. Vera and I were lucky to get the first seats in the bus, giving us a spectacular view of the winding highway and beautiful landscape along the way. This was the beginning of our five-day land tour deep into Alaska's heartland. The city of Anchorage is the largest city in Alaska, with a population of just under three hundred thousand people, and is what they say is the gateway to Alaska adventure. Also, in the background is Mt. Susitna, better known as "Sleeping Lady." It looked great no matter what she was wearing. We stayed overnight, toured the city, and visited the Native Heritage Center and Wildlife Conservation Center.

The next day, we continued the trip on board McKinlay Explorer railcars, going north to Denali National Park. Holland America Line and Princess Cruises own and operate the largest fleet of dome railcars in Alaska, including the McKinlay Explorer. As you might expect, most passengers who travel on these railcars are part of cruise line group tours. McKinley Explorer railcars seat eighty-six to eighty-eight passengers in the upper-level dome. Each passenger has a reserved seat, and the large, curved glass dome windows run the full length of the car, offering superb 360-degree views. Seating is comfortable, with footrests and fold-down tray tables. Each car has its own host guide who provides tour commentary. On the lower level are restrooms, an outdoor viewing platform, and a restaurant. In Denali, we were taken on an eight-hour bus tour of the park, bringing us within fifty miles of Mt. McKinlay's summit of 20,322 feet, the tallest peak in North America. We were very fortunate on this clear day of spring to see the top of Mt. McKinlay, as it is a rare occasion due to rapid weather change at the summit. When we got on the bus, the tour guide instructed us to report any animal sightings by yelling out the directions, such as nine o'clock, twelve o'clock, three o'clock, etc., for everyone to see.

A goal for all visitors is to see a grizzly bear lumbering through the tundra. Denali is home to thirty-nine mammals that vary from shrews to moose. Mostly, we saw wolves, Dall sheep, mountain goats, lynx, coyotes, caribou, and many species of birds, but unfortunately, we did not see grizzly bears on this tour of the park. We spent two nights at the hotel in Denali and then boarded again McKinlay Explorer railcars for the last leg of our trip to Fairbanks before flying home. On the way again, fantastic views from the dome of the railcar expose beautiful landscapes and sightings of wild animals, giving us unforgettable memories to treasure forever.

Fairbanks is the largest city in the interior of Alaska with a population of thirty-two thousand people. During the aurora season (August 21–April 21) in the Fairbanks region, the aurora borealis, also known as the northern lights, almost always appear when the sky is relatively dark and clear. This was the month of May. During the midnight sun season (April 22 –August 20), Fairbanks experiences twenty-four hours of sunlight for seventy days from May 17 to July 27. Imagine that. We had to draw heavy curtains on the windows to make the room dark at night to get some sleep. Fairbanks is known for its rugged beauty and natural wildlife. We enjoyed a tour of the city with stops at several landmarks, including the Trans-Alaska Pipeline, Santa Claus House at the North Pole, and some other well-known points in the city. Also, the Riverboat Discovery tour has with favorite stop at the Trail Breaker Kennel, owned and operated by Susan Butcher, a four-time Iditarod champion, famous for 1,152-mile sled dog racing. We made one more stop at an old gold mine "Gold Dredge #8," where we had a chance to do some panning for gold, which did not produce any favorable results. It was a very cold day, and the best part of this day was when we were served lunch in a wood log cabin. To our surprise, on the menu was moose stew served in metal buckets family style for everyone to take as much as they wanted. I have to say, it was delicious and very hot, great for cold weather. Now on the twelfth day of our Alaska adventure, we were taken to the Fairbanks airport to fly home.

In 2001, Michael and Rani finished their five-year assignment in Charlotte, North Carolina, and returned to the headquarters of the Nuclear Regulatory Commission in Rockville, Maryland. They sold their home in Charlotte and bought another house in Bethesda, not far from their work in Rockville. Even after our retirement, we continued to live in Florida but decided to sell our home in Lighthouse Point and scale down to a much smaller two-bedroom villa in the neighboring town of Deerfield Beach but held on to our rental properties for additional income. Every summer, the trip to Montenegro was on our agenda, where we would spend two to three months on our property there.

Our small house in the village was very interesting with a lot of property around. Greenfields filled with wildflowers and birds singing in the morning would bring back the past of growing up in this place. Yes, those were vacations for us; however, some work had to be done to maintain the property because no one lived there, and we had to close it down for the winter. Fortunately, I am very handy with tools, so I could do many things myself. One of the biggest inconveniences for us was that there was no road coming to the village other than a foot trail, which made it very difficult to shop and bring supplies to the house, so we decided to buy a small used car. The car made our life much easier, even though we had to park about 200 meters away from the house. With the car there, we spent more time on the road, visiting many interesting places in Montenegro. Due to the hot and humid summertime weather, we installed air-conditioning in the house to improve the comfort there that we were used to back home in Florida.

Before my leaving Montenegro in 1959, there were families occupying every house in the village, so it was very active and full of life. Now after fifty years, the village has become one big ruin, with only my cousin Slobodanka living there. The older folks passed away, and the younger ones moved on to the neighboring towns of Petrovac and Budva or elsewhere. Fortunately for us, my house was still livable, so we could use it for short summer vacations. We did this for a few years, and then I got the idea to build the road up to our house in the village, a distance of about 200 meters. What entailed was to widen the foot trail to a minimum of three meters, which required approval of property owners along the way. Perhaps this was more difficult than I could imagine as no one wanted to give up a little of their land, knowing that this would be good for the entire village. I tried very hard to explain to them that when the road came to the village, their land would be worth much more to build on or to sell in the future.

Finally, I was given permission to go ahead with building the road. A few cousins did some help, but I shared the biggest brunt of the expense, which I did not mind because it was good for me and the village too. We liked this arrangement of having summer vacations in Montenegro and spending winters in Florida, which is having the best of both worlds. A few years went by when we got another idea to renovate an old house or to build a new one from scratch. After consultations with a local builder, we decided to demolish the old house and, in its place, go with new construction that would allow new design according to our needs. I signed the contract with the builder with the understanding that I would draw the plans and for him to obtain from the county necessary building permits and complete the entire job for the period of one year.

After signing the contract, Vera and I returned home to Florida, and the construction was going to oversee my brother-in-law, who lived nearby. In the beginning, everything was moving along as planned. I made plans, and the builder demolished the old house, laid down the foundation, and started moving on with the new construction. Halfway through the project, there were some work delays that gave us the feeling that something was not going well. We discovered that the builder was experiencing financial difficulties that created all kinds of problems, not only on our house but also on all other projects that he was undertaking at the time. Since the house was not finished in the time set by the contract, we decided not to go to Montenegro the following year. In the meantime, we had to put some more money into the project and got it completed in 2010. The builder experienced a financial collapse and finally went bankrupt, leaving many projects that he was working on unfinished. To make things worse for us, we discovered that our house was built without building permits, so we could not obtain a certificate of occupancy. Those days in Montenegro, it was common for construction without permits leaving people with problems for the years to come.

To this day, many homes are considered illegal because they were built without proper documentation. I knew, sooner or later, this had to be tackled if we were to legally register our new house. It required to have an architect draw new plans, obtain all necessary documents, pay all the fees, and submit it to the county for approval. All this took lots of money, time, and aggravation that we did not need if the builder obliged the contract that we signed. Cutting corners in construction by not getting permits to dodge required fees is part of the corruption that is going on in Montenegro and all Balkan nations. One can only imagine what process this was, but I was glad to get all this done. We registered the house and obtained the certificate of occupancy.

Now that we have got a beautiful new house, it was important for us to furnish it with things we like. In 2012, we purchased a car and some furnishings in Florida and had them shipped via container to the port of Bar in Montenegro. After shipping them, we flew to Montenegro to be there when the ship arrived. Everything worked out to the plan, and it was time for us to do some travel throughout Europe. Montenegro Airlines was offering five- to six-day tours to many cities in Europe at a very reasonable price, including the flight, hotel, and some local sightseeing. We could not ask for better arrangements, so we booked first the five-day trip to Istanbul, Turkey, where we had a lot to see and do in this beautiful city of 15,636,000 people lying on two continents with the main Bosphorus Bridge connecting the European and Asian sides of Istanbul. We took city tours to see historical sites and monuments, including Camlica Hill, which offers great panoramic views of the city. The hill is the highest one to find the best views of Istanbul from 265 meters above sea level. Next, we went on a city sightseeing cruise with a good view of the Bosphorus Bridge and the surrounding area. Finally, we toured the Hagia Sophia Grand Mosque, which is a major cultural and historical site in Istanbul.

The following year, during our summer vacation in Montenegro, we booked the seven-day tour to Russia to spend three days in St. Petersburg, take an overnight train to Moscow, and stay there for another four days. This was a group of eighteen people from Montenegro with a tour guide that spoke Russian language. We flew from Tivat to St. Petersburg, the second-largest city in Russia, a mecca of cultural, historical, and architectural landmarks. The city is situated on the Neva River, at the head of the Gulf of Finland on the Baltic Sea.

Due to the time essence, our itinerary included only St. Petersburg's major attractions. On the first day, we toured the city and visited the Church of the Savior on Spilled Blood, a Russian Orthodox church that currently functions as a secular museum and church at the same time. The church was founded by the Romanov imperial family and constructed between 1883 and 1907 on the spot where Alexander II was fatally wounded in an assassination attempt on March 1, 1881. This church contains over 7,500 square meters of mosaics, more than any other church in the world. The walls and ceilings inside the church are completely covered in mosaics and biblical scenes of figures.

On the second day, we were taken by tour bus to the town of Pushkin, located 20 kilometers south of St. Petersburg, previously known as Tsarskoye Selo (Tsar's Village), the summer residence of the Russian tsars. The most remarkable landmarks of Pushkin are the majestic Catherine Palace and the magnificent Alexander Palace. On the interior of the palace, each room is decorated with an authentic antique collection, including a great variety of unique artifacts of decorative art, furniture, porcelain, statues, paintings, and more, including personal belongings of Russian emperors and their families. Also, it is worth mentioning the world's famous Amber Room, given as a gift to Peter I by the king of Prussia. The amber panels made from hand-polished pieces of different colors and sizes include frames, garlands, coats of arms, wreaths, monograms, and even entire scenes from the Bible. The palace is surrounded by magnificent, picturesque Catherine Park. We were so overwhelmed with the feelings of all this beauty that will be treasured forever. The last royal residents at the palace were the Romanovs until their tragic deaths in 1918.

On the third and final day in St. Petersburg, we were taken to the Winter Palace, which was the main residence of the Russian Tsars. Magnificently located on the bank of the Neva River, this Baroque-style palace is perhaps St. Petersburg's most impressive attraction. It is also known as the main building of the Hermitage Museum, founded in 1764 by Empress Catherine the Great. The Hermitage is the second-largest museum in the world, with nearly three million items dating from the Stone Age to the present. On the way to the hotel our tour bus drove by legendary warship *Aurora*, docked in St Petersburg as a tourist attraction. *Aurora* was launched on May 11, 1900. During the Bolshevik Revolution of 1917, the cruiser *Aurora* became famous by launching a blank shot, signaling the beginning of the assault on the Winter Palace.

We concluded the three-day tour of St. Petersburg and boarded an overnight sleeper train to Moscow for the distance of 630 kilometers.

Interestingly, we were told that Moscow has nine train stations and one more was in the process of being built. This is the second-largest city in Europe, situated on the Moskva River, with a population of over thirteen million people. We settled in a three-star hotel, Cosmos, located next to the All-Russia Exhibition Center and Memorial Museum of Astronautics, close to Metro and nine kilometers from Red Square.

Due to limited time, our itinerary included only major tourist attractions such as Red Square, Kremlin, St. Basil's, Tretyakov Gallery, Bolshoi Theater, and some personal time. We visited those attractions by tour bus and metro. The tour guide was a Russian lady who lived some time in Montenegro and spoke our language very well.

It was very interesting to see the Kremlin, a complex that's home to the president and tsarist treasures in the armory. Outside its walls is Red Square, Russia's symbolic center. It's home to Lenin's Mausoleum and a burial place for many Soviet leaders. In my time, I heard so much about Red Square and have seen many May Day parades on TV, but I never thought that I would be some day walking and touring this place. Lenin's Mausoleum, also known as Lenin's Tomb, serves as the resting place of Soviet leader Vladimir Lenin, whose preserved body has been on public display since shortly after his death in 1924. We were allowed to enter Lenin's Mausoleum and view the preserved body by slow walking in a single file without stopping. It took some time to digest the meaning of all those historical sights, the culture, and the way of life in Russia. Even before our trip to Russia, we knew that this tour was going to be the most treasured lifetime experience. This was the first time that Vera and I went to a country that was once referred to as "behind Iron Curtain" to find it is still very restrictive in many ways. Even in our hotel, we could not go from the lobby to our room without going through a passport and security check. Four days in Moscow went very fast, and we flew back to Montenegro to spend the rest of our summer vacation there.

For the next several years, we continued with this plan to spend summers in Montenegro and from there, each year, take a tour to a different city in Europe such as Dubrovnik, Ljubljana, Rome, Paris, Madrid, Vienna, Budapest, Prague, and we also booked a cruise from Kotor through many ports in Adriatic to Greece. One year, our friends from Florida, Danilo and Marie Ivancevic, asked us if we were interested in going with them on a twelve-day cruise from Amsterdam to St. Petersburg, covering all Baltic Sea countries. We were very happy to go with them, and since we were already in Montenegro for our summer vacation, we flew from Podgorica to Amsterdam, and they came from Miami the day before boarding our cruise ship. Just happened that our son Michael with Rani were vacationing in Europe, so they also joined us for a day in Amsterdam to spend some time with us.

The city of Amsterdam is the capital of the Netherlands, situated on the river Amstel with a population of a million people. It is known for its artistic heritage, elaborate canal system, and narrow houses with gabled facades, legacies of the city's seventeenth-century golden age. Due to many canals, the city is referred to as the "Venice of the North."

Much of the Netherlands, about a quarter of the country, lies about 6 feet below sea level, so on the edge of the water, there are dikes, and mills pump the water out from the lower land. Since Amsterdam is a seaport, all the ships must pass through the dikes, including the cruise ship that we are just about to sail on. This reminded me of a cruise through the Panama Canal, except that Amsterdam has the world's largest sea lock, measuring five hundred meters long, seventy meters wide, and eighteen meters deep, allowing ships to use the lock 24-7. Finally, we sailed through the locks, and we were on the way to Bremerhaven, Germany, followed by Gdansk, Poland; Riga, Latvia; Tallinn, Estonia; and St. Petersburg, Russia, where we spent two days. This was our second visit to St. Petersburg, and we saw the Hermitage Museum, Tsarskoye Selo, and other interesting sights, but we enjoyed it much more this time because we were with friends. Sailing back from St. Petersburg, we visited Helsinki, Finland; Stockholm, Sweden; and the last port of Copenhagen, Denmark, before coming back to Amsterdam. In each city we visited, there was an abundance of things to do, and we saw that at the end of twelve days, we were exhausted. From the cruise ship, we went directly to the airport for the flight back to Montenegro to finish our summer vacation.

Getting back home in Florida for the winter months always felt like going on another vacation except for needing to maintain our house and the rental property that we were still holding on to. Being away summers did not go very well with our rental properties as we were getting more problems with the tenants, and finding someone to do the repairs while we were gone made us think about selling and ending the rental headaches. We had a friend in real estate who found us a buyer for one building, and the year after, the same person bought the second building, giving us much-needed freedom to travel without rental headaches. Now in Florida, we were left with only one house that we lived in and the other house in the summer place in Montenegro. All this was working for us very well, but realizing that we were getting older and being far away from our son started setting in, and we felt that some decision would have to be made soon about where to spend the last days of our lives.

In Bethesda, Maryland, next door to our son, lived an older couple that was very friendly with Michael and Rani. With our high hopes, we kept an eye on that house if it ever came on the market to buy it. After their passing, the relatives notified Michael that the house was available for sale, so a decision had to be made immediately to avoid real estate listing. We gave Michael the power of attorney to agree on the price and to proceed with the purchase of the house. This happened in April of 2017, just before our trip to Montenegro. In prior years, we always flew from Miami to Montenegro, but this year, we came to Washington first, came to see the house, stayed for a week, and then went on to Montenegro for another summer vacation. The house was in very good condition but needed lots of work. On the first floor was the living area, screened porch, and attached garage, while upstairs were the bedrooms. Michael suggested that in place of a screened porch, we built an addition for the master's bedroom and bathroom to make it more convenient for us at the old age. We liked that idea very much, so Michael hired an architect to draw plans and then look for a builder to construct this addition to the house. This project was to add approximately four hundred square feet to the house built to the latest standards and local building codes. We knew what we wanted, and the architect gave us some good suggestions to get the project on the way. We went on to Montenegro without any worry because Michael was overseeing all the activities. We were very lucky that this addition to the house did not have to be done in a hurry because the architect was very slow in producing the plans. Like all other years, taking short trips from Montenegro, this year we picked a five-day excursion to Madrid, Spain. We toured the city and enjoyed all the highlights and, of course, delicious tapas in many bars. It was very hot weather during our stay, but very well worth the trip. Another summer vacation was coming to an end, and we went back to Florida while still working on our additional plans that were not finalized until February 2018.

On March 2, we got word of an incident that happened at our newly purchased home in Bethesda. The storm in the area with high winds caused a huge tree from the neighbors in the back of our house to fall on the house next to us, demolishing it and slightly damaging the porch of our house. Thank God no one was home next door when that happened, and fortunately, we had good insurance to cover the damage to our property. Anyway, it did not affect us very much because the porch had to be demolished to make room for the new addition. Prior to submitting plans to the Building department for a permit, we had to select the builder to do the construction of our new addition to the house. The timing worked out very well for us. We made a trip to Bethesda, selected the contractor, stayed for a month, and then went to Montenegro for summer vacation.

The house there needed some attention too. Since it was very difficult to find laborers, I ended up doing most of the work myself. In the past several years, there was a big transformation of Montenegro's cities and towns with the eruption of new construction, mostly along the Adriatic Sea. With all new hotels and apartment houses being built, there were no new roads to accommodate the large influx of tourists, which created monumental traffic jams during the summer months, just when we were there. It helped that our house was in the village, but whenever we had to go somewhere, we had to cope with the traffic situation, which we did not like at all. In addition to the traffic situation, many other things were getting in the way of our rest and relaxation as in the previous years. Perhaps, getting older, the long flights to and from Montenegro did not help the situation, so Vera and I started thinking about selling the house in the village. It was very hard for me to even think about selling the house that I was born in, but reality was setting in that helped me go forward with this decision. One other and perhaps the most important reason to sell the house was that our son Michael was born in America and would not be going there as we did, and there were no grandchildren to inherit it. We listed our house with several real estate agencies in the area, but through the summer and winter of 2018, it did not produce any potential buyers, so we rest our hopes for the following year when we return to Montenegro.

On the way back to the US, we spent some time in Bethesda to see the progress on the construction of the addition to our newly purchased house. The contractor knew that we were not moving in anytime soon, so the work progress was very slow but moving forward. After a few weeks in Bethesda, we returned to Florida for the winter months. Being away from Florida the whole summer, we missed our friends there, and I think they were happy to see us back. Our friends loved to come to our house and enjoy delicious dinners that Vera always prepared as she was getting famous. Some of our friends that we met through the church were seasonal that we called them "snowbirds," spending winters in Florida and summers up north, while others lived in Florida all year-round.

The following year, 2019, we decided to make our trip to Montenegro early in the spring and come back middle of August to be in Bethesda when the work on our house was all done. This time, we drove our car to Bethesda so we could take some important things with us to the new house there. Also, we wanted to spend a few extra days on the road to visit Charleston, South Carolina, and Richmond, Virginia. A long time ago, we visited Charleston but wanted to see this port city again with its beautiful cobblestone streets, horse-drawn carriages, and pastel antebellum houses, particularly in the elegant French Quarter and Battery districts. Also, we enjoyed the Battery Promenade and Waterfront Park, both overlooking Charleston Harbor.

We spent two nights in Charleston and another night in Richmond, Virginia, before returning to Bethesda.

Everything worked out to the plan, and we were on our way to Montenegro early in the spring. As far as we are concerned, it is the best time of the year when wildflowers are blooming, the birds are singing, and, as they say, it is spring in the air. The rugged landscapes of the Montenegrin coast, in the spring, are interspersed with shrubs of a beautiful plant of robust and yellow color—Žuka (Spartium Junceum), which gives an attractive, colorful decoration to the hilly configuration of the coastal terrain and provides the air with a note of its pleasant and unobtrusive scent. It is a real treasure to enjoy the colors and smells of nature.

This year, our stay in Montenegro was much shorter, so we did not plan any trips outside the country as we did all the years before. Also, there were no potential buyers for our house, so in August, we returned to Bethesda and, after two weeks, drove back to Florida. Once again, we were faced with another decision to make as we realized that having the house in three places is getting to be more difficult to maintain and get to and from. Whenever Vera and I had to decide on something, we would analyze the situation that we were in, decide on, and go after to accomplish it. This time was no different. The decision was to sell the house in Florida and move permanently to a newly purchased and renovated home in Bethesda.

At the end of September 2019, the house was on the market and listed with the same agent that we bought it from. We lived in a very popular area, practically on the golf course, with a lot of privacy and close to everything.

With no surprise to us, two weeks after the listing, we had a potential buyer with a reasonable offer that we accepted, and the purchase contract was signed. Once we had the contract, the buyer moved on to getting inspections and all other procedures needed so we could set a date for the final closing. For us, the most important thing was to prepare the house for new occupants, meaning to move out before the closing date. We hired the moving company to move only select pieces of furniture as we had already partially furnished our new home in Bethesda. Vera was not comfortable with that moving company packing and moving the crystal and kitchenware, so we packed it ourselves and rented a one-way small U-Haul truck, drew it to Bethesda, and returned to Florida by plane. Anyone selling the house knows that this process is not an easy one, especially in our age. Fortunately for us, we had lots of experience through the years by selling several homes, including our rental properties. Our house was in excellent condition, so everything was moving along without any problem, and the closing date was set for November 19, 2019.

In the meantime, we started seeing friends for final goodbyes. Living and working in South Florida for fifty years, we had a large network of friends that was very hard to walk away from. We liked Florida and the people we were with, so our emotions ran high as we entered another chapter of our lives. Last night in South Florida, we stayed in the hotel, and the next day, we had lunch with close friends and then drove up to Daytona Beach to spend the night. We wanted to take it easy on the road, so the second night, we stayed in Fayetteville, North Carolina.

Finally, we arrived in Bethesda, our new home from now on. Looking back, over the past two and a half months, we have achieved so much. Going through the sale of the house, moving out of South Florida, and saying goodbyes to many friends was very stressful and exhausting for us, but then we had a lot of time to rest and reflect on all this. Moving to a great suburb of Bethesda gave us good privacy and yet being close to everything but most important of all was having the house next door to our son and daughter-in-law. This was the time when the COVID-19 pandemic was on the rise in the United States, making our everyday lives more difficult with many restrictions imposed upon us. The Trump administration also issued many restrictions for people traveling to and from the United States that affected all of us. Faced with this situation, we canceled our plans for Montenegro's summer vacation of 2020 and decided to wait for vaccination approval with the hope of better days ahead. This pandemic has affected the public's mental health and well-being in a variety of ways, through isolation and loneliness, job loss, and financial instability. Personally, I was worried because Vera and I, as senior citizens, were in the most critical group to be infected with the virus. Fortunately, we were in good health, and it was not until January 2021 that we got the first dose of the vaccine, followed by a second dose in February. It was only then that we were breathing a little easier, knowing with more people being vaccinated, the situation would get better. Some states and local governments maintained vaccination or masking orders for public employees and health care workers into 2023, but almost all such mandates had lapsed by May 11.

During my lifetime, I do not remember any epidemic being this serious and taking so many lives for such a long time. In 2021, the situation was getting a little better, but not anywhere near the end. We decided to make a trip to Montenegro later in the summer, giving us more time for the situation to somewhat improve. No one could get to the airport without wearing a face mask and having a record of vaccination. For the duration of the entire flight, we had to wear masks except for the time of eating or drinking. We got to Montenegro at the beginning of August, and as far as COVID-19 was concerned, the situation was about the same as anywhere else in the world except for the people there being very relaxed and, for the most part, not obeying the restrictions.

Our house there was closed for almost two years and required some maintenance as well as good cleaning. It was still on the market, so it was another reason to have it in the best possible shape with the hope of producing a potential buyer before our return home to Bethesda. The location of the house is about a five-minute drive to Petrovac and ten minutes to St. Stefan, with a spectacular view of the Adriatic Sea, making it very desirable for small families. A few years back, the prospective buyers were mostly Russian tourists, but gradually, a political climate changed, and more laws were passed favoring European Union country investors, so there was an increase in British and German real estate buyers.

Our house built in 2010.

Toward the end of August, we started getting calls from the real estate agencies to show our house, so the interest was there, and our hopes were high. This went on for a while, and finally, toward the end of September, one German couple showed an interest in our house. When they came back for the second and third time, we knew that they liked the house and might make an offer.

There were many homes for sale in this area, but some of them were not properly registered or were built without permits, creating big problems for the buyers. As they say, Vera and I had all our ducks in a row, meaning that our house was properly registered, had an occupancy permit, and all fees were paid, making it free and clear for the change of ownership. I believe that all this helped the buyer decide and come up with an offer that we accepted. On October 4, 2021, the last day before our return home, we met with the buyer in the notary office in Budva to sign the contract with the stipulation that we return in January to close the deal. The buyer forwarded 10 percent of the proceeds to our bank in Montenegro and the balance of sale would come on the closing day in January of 2022. Once again, we were under a lot of stress by selling another property, but at the same time very happy that everything was moving forward. Flying back home with a contract in our hands, we considered it as a great accomplishment.

Mike and Rani were proud of us for getting so much done in a short time. The pressure was still on because we had to return to Montenegro in January to finalize the sale. However, the next three months were just what we needed for some much-deserved rest and relaxation. It went much faster than we thought, so we set a date for January 16, 2022, to fly from Washington, DC, to Podgorica via Vienna. I just knew that somewhere along the line, we would encounter some problems, but I never gave a thought that this was the wintertime and the weather might play a part in our travel schedule. The weather prediction for January 16 was light snow toward the end of the day, and our hope was that we would get out without any problem. The airline was Austrian Air, and their assessment was also that everything would be fine. We boarded the plane on time and moved on toward the runway, where the plane had to get in line for deicing before departure. The snow was piling on much faster than anticipated, so the situation got worse by the minute. Apparently, there was a problem with a deicing crew that was not adequately prepared to handle so many planes, causing delays for hours. At the end of four hours at the runway, we got an announcement from the captain that the plane was returning to the hangar and the flight was canceled. The airline crew placed us overnight in a local hotel with instructions to return the next morning to reschedule of our departure. It was late in the night, and everyone was tired and frustrated, but there was nothing we could do to help the situation we were in. The next morning, we got to the airport and waited until early afternoon when, finally, we boarded the plane and flew out. Getting to Vienna in the late hours of the night, we had to wait for the morning to find out information for our connecting flight to Podgorica. Throughout the day, the airline posted that our connecting flight was delayed, and after nine hours, we found out that the flight was canceled due to weather conditions at Podgorica airport. The next day was the same story, so after spending two nights in Vienna, we finally arrived in Montenegro. This was one of the most difficult trips we ever had, taking four days and three nights to travel from Washington, DC, to Podgorica, Montenegro. Despite all the difficulties we encountered on this trip, we were happy at last to be there in time to prepare the house for the new occupant.

At the end of January, the buyer was coming from Germany with a moving company delivering his furniture directly into our house. Everything worked out as planned, so Vera and I moved to a hotel in Budva for the rest of our stay in Montenegro. On February 4, 2022, we had closing, and finally, the sale of the house was behind us. The remaining property that was not part of the sale with the house, I assigned it to my first cousin Gojko's two sons, Simo and Velimir (Vanja), leaving me free and clear of all assets in Montenegro.

Our return flight was scheduled for February 19, giving us enough time to get some rest and visit relatives for a final goodbye. Some relatives we visited, and others came to our hotel, so the time was moving along very fast. Last few days before our trip back home, I was under unexplainable stress and tensions that were building up in me. Perhaps it was the realization that I might never return to this land that I loved so much. On the last day, we went to the cemetery to visit the graves of departed loved ones. When I approached our family grave and Uncle Spiro's and Aunt Maria's, I screamed loudly and burst into tears. It was building up in me for the last few days, and finally, I broke down crying. Vera was not in much better shape, but she hugged me with comforting words, and it took some time until I pulled myself together. It seems to me that these moments left a mark on my life, so now when I am writing about this almost two years later, without realizing it, the emotions came back, and the tears came down my face.

On February 19, 2022, we returned home to Bethesda to give full attention to our lives and enjoy every minute that we have left in the remainder of our lives. The coronavirus was still with us, and the restrictions did not end in the US until May of 2023. After the restrictions were lifted, there was overwhelming relief for the people to start rebuilding their lives. We were still cautious and stayed close to home for most of the summer, but we got an idea to make another trip to Europe in the month of September, where we spent twenty-two days in Montenegro and six days in Barcelona, Spain. This entire trip was very enjoyable and much more different from any other trip we previously took to Montenegro. Since we did not have a house there anymore, we checked in at Hotel Palas in Petrovac, and for the first time, I felt being a tourist, enjoying every minute of our stay. In Barcelona, we were delighted with many tourist attractions to see in and out of the city. This Mediterranean city is very popular for cruise ships to visit, which adds up to the tourist congestion that we did cope with quite well. As they say, all good things must come to an end, so did our vacation too. Coming back home to a pleasant surprise of our life. Our son Michael (Mike) is a recipient of a Distinguished Executive 2023 Presidential Award. As a matter of public records, he waited to tell us after the US Office of Personnel Management released the list of 2023 Presidential Award Recipients of various departments in the US government, and Michael is from the Nuclear Regulatory Commission. After receiving a bachelor's degree in nuclear engineering from the University of Florida, he went on to a master's degree in reliability engineering from the University of Maryland with a concentration in probabilistic risk analysis. He is also a graduate of the NRC's SES Candidate Development Program. Michael joined the US Nuclear Regulatory Commission (NRC) in 1990 as a general engineer in NRR. Since joining the NRC, he has held numerous staff positions. Currently, Michael is serving as the director of the Division of Risk Assessment, Office of Nuclear Reactor Regulation (NRR), and has held that position since January 2018. Vera and I could not be prouder of Michael and his achievements.

By the time I finish this book, I will be eighty-four years old and, if I may say, still in good condition. I do not regret anything that I have done in my life, but if I could relive past years, I would most certainly like to devote more of my time to Vera and Michael. After all, the way I see it, the family should be the most important in everyone's life. Looking back on my life to this very day, it was one constant moving fast forward in all directions. From now on, I feel my life is in God's hands, waiting for that final sunset.

About the Author

Branko Franovick was born on March 1, 1940, in a small village of today's Montenegro. One can only imagine the conditions of growing up during World War II in a war-torn country, losing father in the war and later mother remarrying, finishing elementary school there, and after five years, immigrating to the United States of America.

He served in the Armed Forces, became a citizen of the United States, returned to his native land of Montenegro, and got married to a sweetheart from childhood. He was employed in a metal stamping company, enrolling in the night school with the final goal of becoming a mechanical engineer.

After forty-six years of employment with many accomplishments along the way, he retired to enjoy golden years and write this book, *The Journey of My Life*, to record lifelong memories and overcome struggles and obstacles to achieve a better life.